THE LEGO® TRAINS BOOK

THE LEGO® TRAINS BOOK

HOLGER MATTHES

no starch
press

SAN FRANCISCO

The LEGO® Trains Book. Copyright © 2017 by No Starch Press.

The LEGO Trains Book is a translation of the German original, *LEGO®-Eisenbahn*, copyright © 2016 by dpunkt.verlag GmbH, Heidelberg, Germany.

Printed in China

First Printing

21 20 19 18 17   1 2 3 4 5 6 7 8 9

ISBN-10: 1-59327-819-5
ISBN-13: 978-1-59327-819-9

Publisher: William Pollock
Production Editor: Riley Hoffman
Cover Design: Max Burger
Interior Design: Beth Middleworth
Photography: Andreas Bahler
Developmental Editor: Tyler Ortman
Translator: Ronald Vallenduuk
Technical Reviewer: Michael Gale
Copyeditor: Rachel Monaghan
Compositors: Riley Hoffman and Max Burger
Proofreader: Shannon Waite
Indexing: BIM Creatives, LLC

The images on the following pages are used with permission: page 43 (top) © Roland Dahl; pages 74 and 103 © Michael Gale; pages 110 and 117 (top) © Siemens (*www.siemens.com/press*); page 114 (top) © Luis Rentero; page 124 (bottom) © Jürgen Heegmann; page 126 (template) © Ralf Hiesgen (*www.lok13.de*); page 134 © Steffen Rau.

For information on distribution, translations, or bulk sales, please contact No Starch Press, Inc. directly:

No Starch Press, Inc.
245 8th Street, San Francisco, CA 94103
phone: 1.415.863.9900; info@nostarch.com; www.nostarch.com

Library of Congress Control Number: 2017943793

Production Date: 6.20.17
Plant & Location: Printed in Guangdong Province, China
Job/Batch #: 79510-0

CONTENTS

ACKNOWLEDGMENTS

On the occasion of the 50th anniversary of LEGO trains in 2016, I published my first book: *LEGO Eisenbahn: Konzepte und Techniken für realistische Modelle*. Now, the English version, *The LEGO Trains Book*, is available. After Jake McKee's book *Getting Started with LEGO Trains*, this is only the second book entirely dedicated to LEGO railways and building your own train models.

I could not have made this book without the support, direct and indirect, from many people that I would like to thank here.

First, I must mention Gabriel Neumann from dpunkt.verlag, who came up with the idea and gave me the opportunity to create the book. Another big thank you goes to Tyler Ortman and Riley Hoffman from No Starch Press, who worked hard to make this book available for the international audience. This English version wouldn't have been possible without Ronald Vallenduuk's translation and Michael Gale's reviews. Both contributed their expertise to make this book a great resource for all LEGO train fans.

Thanks also to the numerous LEGO fans around the globe who create their MOCs and present them online. Even as a longstanding LEGO fan, I still regularly wonder how certain details were created, and I am always fascinated to see new creations.

Thank you to BrickLink shops big and small who supply me with the raw materials and who, by parting out many sets, make it possible to acquire large quantities of certain parts.

Thank you to all the invisible volunteers in the LEGO fan community who contribute to the various databases such as the parts catalog on BrickLink, and the programmers and parts authors who create and update the open source virtual building programs. Without them, it would have been impossible to create my own building instructions.

A personal thank you to the photographers who let me use their pictures to create a link with the real world. These photographers are Jürgen Heegmann, Ralf Hiesgen, Steffen Rau, Luis Rentero, Armin Schwarz, and Siemens AG (*www.siemens.com/press*).

Special thanks go to Roland Dahl, who patiently answered all my questions about rendering images in POV-Ray, gave me many tips, and brought the Monorail picture to life.

Many thanks to my friends and family. They motivated me, kept an interest throughout the process, and very importantly, cast a critical eye on the developing book.

The biggest thank you goes out to my old friend and master photographer Andy Bahler (*www.andybahler.de*), without whose pictures this book would have been useless. His commitment, night after night, was above and beyond expectation, and the undiscovered broken coupling on the 7740 brought him right back into my LEGO world. Thanks, Andy!

Enjoy the book, and build!

Holger Matthes
www.holgermatthes.de/bricks

Andy Bahler at work

FOREWORD

For as long as I can remember, I have always been a train fan. As with many children bitten by the same bug, I would indulge in any opportunity to watch, ride, or play with trains. Playing with trains progressively evolved into the more serious hobby of model trains. Building with LEGO bricks was also a big part of my childhood. I would build towns, spaceships, vehicles, aircraft, or whatever took my fancy. The LEGO system allowed me to explore more creative and freeform building experiences distinct from the more rigid and disciplined world of scale model trains.

For many years into my adulthood, my hobby time was dominated by model trains. But despite my focus on model trains, I had the presence of mind to retain my childhood LEGO collection. This proved to be a good decision, since I was able to introduce that LEGO collection to my children. This marked the beginning of what was to become a new era of my life with the LEGO hobby.

The "Fairy Bricks Express," a MOC that I contributed to the Fairy Bricks charity auction event at BRICK 2015 in London. This model was my first serious attempt at building a LEGO train and is based on the British Rail Inter-City 125—one of my all-time favorite trains.

Building with my children rekindled the joy of endless hours of freeform building and exploration that I enjoyed as a child. It wasn't long before I found myself attempting to build LEGO trains. My early attempts were basic, but my scale model train instincts suggested that better results were possible, especially with the broad range of new LEGO parts that hadn't existed in my childhood.

I started to explore the internet for inspiration and to see if there was a contemporary LEGO train hobby or community. I quickly discovered that there was in fact a very active and accomplished building community. Furthermore, the standard of the models I was seeing was beginning to approach the fidelity of traditional scale model trains. I recall this being a "light bulb" moment for me—a realization that I could merge my two lifelong hobby interests into a combined passion for building model trains using the medium of LEGO bricks.

When exploring the LEGO train hobby, it doesn't take long before you come across the name Holger Matthes. His epic and groundbreaking creations vividly demonstrate the art of the possible. Furthermore, Holger has taken the time to document and describe all the useful and creative building techniques specific to LEGO train builders. I owe Holger a debt of gratitude for the knowledge and inspiration that guided my progression through this hobby. In this context, it was almost surreal that a few years later, I found myself being asked to review and make a small contribution to this book.

In the pages that follow, you will find the collective wealth of wisdom gathered over many years. This is the book LEGO train builders everywhere have been missing. It will prove to be an invaluable resource and reference for all train builders—beginners and experts alike. Lastly, it will provide a source of inspiration and hopefully encourage newcomers to take the plunge and discover the joy of LEGO trains!

Michael Gale

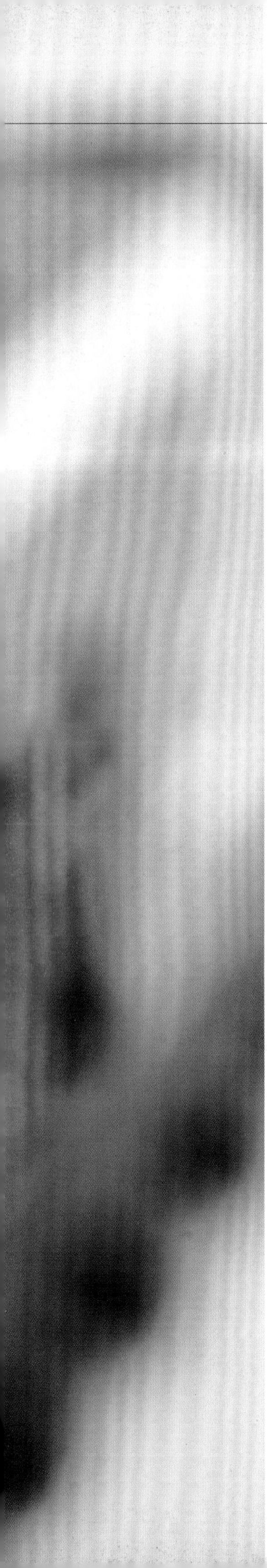

INTRO DUC TION

Decades ago, the toy designers at LEGO likely never imagined how durable their work would be. Today, parents can dust off their childhood LEGO trains and play together with their children who have just received their first brand-new LEGO train set. And fans of all ages can revive older sets and parts to create entirely new models.

Model trains in LEGO

This book is about designing LEGO trains. The first part of the book gives an overview of LEGO trains over the different eras, covers some history, and answers questions about how to combine old LEGO trains from the attic with today's kits.

The second part of the book is about building your own LEGO train models, also known as *My Own Creations (MOCs)*. Using my many years of experience building LEGO models, I'll show you how to create proper train models, covering both the possibilities and the limitations.

Finally, the book ends with step-by-step building instructions for several models.

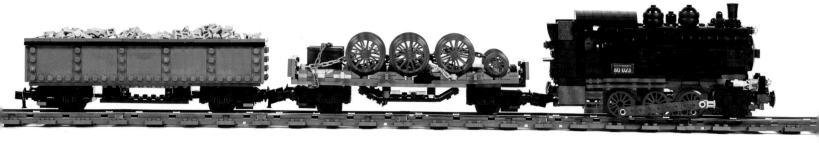

ADVICE BEFORE YOU START

LEGO fans like to dream up their own models, plan them, build them, and eventually document and display them. Fans use parts from various sources for their creations. It's a labor of love, and most do not want to think about the actual cost of a model in parts and time. Suffice it to say that a train MOC is much more expensive than an official LEGO set of similar size.

If you're just discovering the hobby, remember that not everyone has the time and ability to create professional-looking instructions for their models. Be inspired, respect other people's creative efforts, and get creative yourself—even if there are no building instructions available for your dream model or you don't have all the right pieces in your collection.

LEGO ON THE INTERNET

It's hard to imagine the LEGO hobby without the internet. Whether you are working with your old train sets from the attic or starting to build your own creations, the internet is a valuable resource. There is an endless supply of inspiring pictures and videos from fans on sites like Flickr and YouTube, and those same sites will allow you to share your own creations with the world. By connecting with other fans, you can get answers to your questions, learn new building techniques, find sources for parts, and more. You may even discover a LEGO club in your area where you can meet other fans in person.

In this section, I'll introduce a few major sites that every LEGO fan should be familiar with: the official LEGO site, BrickLink, and Brickset.

MOC on rails

THE OFFICIAL LEGO WEBSITE

At the official LEGO website (*www.lego.com*), you'll find information about the current product range. The online shop (*shop.lego.com*) offers some exclusive sets that are not available in regular shops, and you can buy individual pieces from a regularly changing selection of parts in the Pick A Brick section.

Current parts can also be ordered in limited amounts through Customer Service (*service.lego.com*). When ordering a part, it helps to have its *Element ID*, a unique identification number that defines the shape and color of a part. You can find this Element ID in the building instructions, which are available from the official LEGO site and in set inventories on Brickset.

BRICKLINK

BrickLink (*www.bricklink.com*) is a portal for hundreds of online shops that sell LEGO sets, parts, building instructions, and other related items.

BrickLink parts catalog

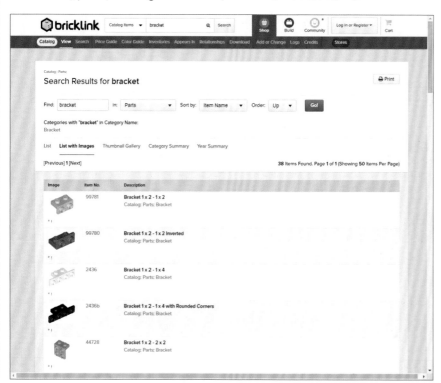

Additionally, BrickLink hosts the most complete database of LEGO parts and sets, including parts and colors that have long been discontinued. Parts are also sometimes redesigned, and BrickLink lists the different versions.

Two variations of the 1×1 plate with light clip

You can browse or search the BrickLink catalog by sets, parts, or themes. As a reader of this book, you'll probably find the Trains theme of interest. For people new to the hobby, the parts catalog is a good place to learn what's available. Searching for an unusual part by its ID number can also be a good way to identify an old set.

BRICKSET

Brickset (*www.brickset.com*) is primarily a database of LEGO sets. There, you can find information about almost every LEGO set ever released, organized by theme and year. The information available for older sets is not always as detailed as what is available for recent sets, but there are links to other LEGO information websites to fill in the gaps.

Brickset database

In addition to the database, the Brickset site offers set reviews and LEGO news from around the world. You can also register for a free account to track your collection of LEGO sets as well as your wishlist.

NAMING SETS AND ELEMENTS IN THIS BOOK

Official LEGO sets in the book are identified by their set number preceded by a hash mark (for example, #7750). Parts are named according to the fan-created BrickLink classification system, which has become the de facto worldwide standard. The LEGO Group uses its own system for naming parts and colors, but that system ignores parts that are no longer in production. Fans prefer the BrickLink system, which covers all parts and colors, old and new.

The available range of elements is constantly changing, and parts and colors come and go. Sometimes a part was used only in a single set that was produced for just two or three years. A lot of those parts can still be found on the secondhand market, in particular on BrickLink.

Parts labeled *HTF* (*hard to find*) are rare because they have never been used in official sets.

A NOTE ON DIFFICULTY

The models in this book vary in level of difficulty. Some of them set the bar high and show what is possible with LEGO. Not only is building these models difficult, but they also use parts in colors that are difficult to find and may be expensive. This is LEGO, though, so there are always many ways to solve a problem. If you can't build it exactly as it's shown, use your imagination and creativity to build it with the parts you have available.

LET'S GET STARTED!

I hope you will enjoy discovering (or rediscovering) your LEGO hobby and the exciting world of LEGO trains.

The author in his workshop

A HISTORY OF LEGO TRAINS

Let's explore the evolution of the
LEGO train systems from the
earliest set to the present.

Since their creation, trains have been a small theme in the LEGO universe, with some fans seeing the theme only as an extension of LEGO Town or City. Nevertheless, the LEGO Group has continually improved its trains over the years.

Just as old and new bricks fit together, older and newer LEGO trains are compatible. This is because the *gauge*, or width, of the track has remained the same year after year. What's changed is how LEGO trains are powered.

The earliest LEGO trains were released in 1966, beginning the *Blue Era*. This era included unpowered trains, 4.5 V battery-powered trains, and a 12 V power system. This system maintained the same plastic running rails but introduced a clever inner metal rail placed between the plastic rails. This adaptation allows unpowered, 4.5 V powered, and 12 V powered trains to seamlessly share the same track. In 1980, the *Gray Era* introduced improvements to the power components, as well as new gray track.

Locomotive with motor from an early set (#112)

A decade later, LEGO completely changed the architecture of the train system by introducing all-metal track components powered by a new 9 V electrical system. By 2006, this 9 V metal track system was replaced by the more economical plastic RC track system. The plastic RC track was nearly identical to (and compatible with) the metal 9 V track it replaced. Today's Power Functions trains have reverted to battery-powered operation but can be controlled remotely by infrared.

This chapter gives an overview of the various eras of LEGO trains, their key components, and how they fit together.

Four decades lie between the oldest (#182, right) and newest (#10233, left) LEGO train sets in this lineup.

THE BLUE ERA (1966–1979)

Fifty years ago, the LEGO product range looked quite different than it does today. Only standard bricks were available, and only in a primary color palette. LEGO had just started manufacturing wheels, and the minifigure had not yet been invented.

The very first train set (#323), introduced in 1964, predates the Blue Era. It used parts available at the time and did not include rails. Blue rails were eventually introduced, with white 2×8 plates as crossties. Along with red wheels, those blue rails and white crossties are the signature look of the Blue Era.

POWER SOURCES

Blue Era sets can be divided into three categories—"push" trains with no motor, trains with a 4.5 V motor powered by batteries, and trains with a 12 V motor powered by an electrified rail.

Even back then, LEGO designers envisaged a railway system that could grow with its young owners, so some of the push-along locomotives can be upgraded with the addition of a motor.

The train motor for both the 4.5 V and the 12 V systems is a small electric motor packaged with some gearing in a bulky studded housing. Those studs allow a locomotive to be built around the motor housing. The driving wheels have metal axles that click into the motor.

My first train set (#182) has the classic Blue Era design.

4.5 V BATTERY-POWERED SYSTEM

Power for the 4.5 V motors is supplied by three C batteries housed either in a bulky battery box or in a special battery car. The battery car is usually dressed as a tender or freight car and coupled directly behind the engine with a cable connecting the batteries to the motor.

A 4.5 V motor (left) with battery car trailing behind

To operate the train, there is a switch on the battery box. The three positions are forward, backward, and off. That means there's no speed control—but that's hardly an issue given the crawling pace of these trains.

Train direction switch

Despite the lack of speed control, this system did offer some clever components designed to enhance its play value:

- A train direction switch, which looks like a short post next to the track. When the post pushes the switch on a passing train's battery car, the train reverses direction.
- The mechanical stop signal (#156) has a plate between the rails that, in its raised stop position, pushes a button underneath the battery car, breaking the circuit and stopping the train.
- The electronic whistle system (included in sets #118, #138, and #139) consists of a whistle and small controller with integrated microphone. The controller's microphone detects when the whistle is blown and reverses the direction of the train.

12 V ELECTRIFIED RAIL SYSTEM

There was only so much fun to be had with a crawling 4.5 V train. The Blue Era also saw the first trains powered by electrified rail—the first 12 V trains. The extra power of the 12 V system is noticeable; it makes the trains go much faster. The speed of the train is controlled by a blue transformer with a red knob that fits the color scheme of the era.

The Blue Era transformer controls the speed of the train.

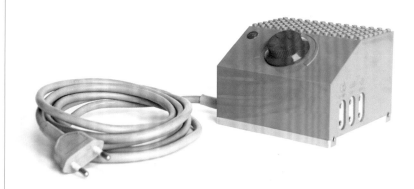

Electrical contacts underneath the train motor connect with the metal rail. Regular straight and curved track pieces from the 4.5 V sets could easily be adapted to the 12 V system with the addition of a metal rail, but switches and crossings without metal rails cannot be upgraded in this way.

TRACKS

The basic track pieces from the 1960s remain unchanged, so a Power Functions train you buy today can run on the old Blue Era track. Unfortunately, anyone familiar with the world of model railways will find the selection of tracks across all eras of LEGO trains to be woefully limited, despite requests from LEGO train fans for more complex geometries.

STRAIGHT TRACK

Straight rails (#156) are 16 studs (5 inches) long and are fixed 6 studs apart on white 2×8 plates that act as crossties. The rail's ribbed texture increases the friction of the rail against a motorized train wheel. This gives motor-powered trains better traction and lowers the risk of wheel slip. Upgrading to 12 V is as simple as adding the powered metal rails (#750).

Rails and crossties are connected by single studs at each end of the rails, making the connection rather fragile and frustrating for children to play with. Builders can achieve more stability by placing another 2×8 plate halfway between rail connections.

CURVED TRACK

Curved track is also built from single rails (#157). The shorter inside rail has a smooth surface, while the longer outside rail has a ribbed surface like the straight rails. All LEGO curved segments have the same geometry—16 segments make up a full circle that has a radius of 40 studs (12.6 inches) measured to the middle of the track (between the inner and outer rails).

A track layout with these dimensions fits nicely in a child's bedroom but poses a challenge for ambitious LEGO railway hobbyists.

12 V track in the Blue Era

Straight track from the Blue Era, with a stop signal (#156)

Curved track from the Blue Era

Hand-operated 4.5 V switch from the Blue Era

SWITCHES

Switches for LEGO railways are produced in left-handed or right-handed versions, allowing the train to "turn out" on a parallel line of track. The Blue Era offered three options: hand-operated switches for 4.5 V (#154), hand-operated switches for 12 V (#755), and remote-controlled switches for 12 V (#753 and #754).

The diverging track runs alongside the main straight track with the cross-ties of both tracks nearly touching each other. Locomotives and wide cars can run on a collision course using the switch. But the switch allows for compact track arrangements, as well.

4.5 V crossing from the Blue Era

CROSSINGS

Crossings allow for variety in track design and help you fit as much track as possible in a small space. Both the 4.5 V (#155) and the 12 V (#756) versions are 16 studs long, crossing at a 90-degree angle. In real life, these crossings are very rare, but they're great for acting out railway catastrophes.

OTHER ELEMENTS

The birth of LEGO trains also saw the development of specialized elements. Many of these parts are still used in MOCs today.

Typical elements from the Blue Era

WHEELS

Train wheels in the Blue Era are mostly red, although some were produced in black toward the end of the era. They come in one size. If they are not fixed to the train base, they can be connected to special 2×4 bricks with axles.

Although the size is the same, locomotive wheels and car wheels have different profiles and different styles, with spokes or studs.

For small steam engines (#133, #725), there are connecting rods that can be attached to the center stud of a train wheel.

Blue Era wheels

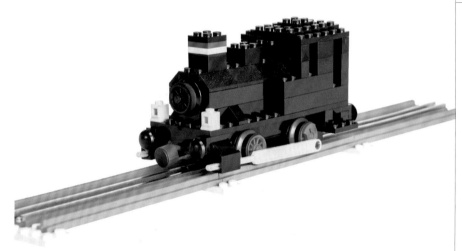

Blue Era engine (#133/#725) with connecting rods

TRAIN BASES

Locomotives and cars are mostly built on ready-made train bases. These bases have fixed axles and coupling magnets. For engines, there are also 6×16 plates with a hole in the middle that accommodates the train's motor.

Train bases for locomotives and cars

Blue Era truck

TRUCKS

Trucks (also known as *bogies*) are the subframes on train wheel systems that allow trains to take curves by pivoting relative to the main chassis. For LEGO trains, they aren't always necessary. Nearly all engines and cars of this era are very short and have two axles, which are fixed to the train base. There are a few exceptions, including longer cars on trucks (#113) that use a bulky 4×4×1 part as the turntable for the trucks.

COUPLINGS AND BUFFERS

The earliest LEGO train couplings were simple hooks, but these were soon replaced by magnets, and that system remains in use today. These magnets are usually fixed to the train base, and the red or blue housing of the magnets indicates the polarity. The pivot point of the magnets is the only articulation point between locomotives and cars—except when trucks are used.

Blue Era buffer pieces

Individual buffer pieces mount underneath the long train base.

WINDOWS

The small train window is a noteworthy and handsome part, and it is still a popular part to use in MOCs.

An old window still has its uses today.

SEEN FROM TODAY'S PERSPECTIVE

The Blue Era will bring back many childhood memories for older generations. Most questions I get about the Blue Era indicate that many "attic finds" are incomplete or broken. The electronic components in particular have not withstood the test of time—a battery car with leaky battery acid cannot be revived.

That said, Blue Era motors are relatively easy to repair. Inside, you will find many non-LEGO parts, and replacement parts are still available from BrickLink. The old 4.5 V trains can run as a heritage railway on modern track layouts. And with a little creativity, the 4.5 V components can be replaced with Power Functions ones.

Still, the Blue Era has little to offer children and newcomers. The blue track with its single-stud connections is fragile, and the lackluster performance of the 4.5 V trains and high rolling friction of the old train wheels make them not much fun to play with.

Summary: Blue Era 4.5 V Battery System

Power	Three 1.5 V (C) batteries in battery car, 4.5 V train motor (#107 and others)
Track	Blue single plastic rails, white crossties (2×8 plates)
Sets	Train sets (#182 and others) as well as separate locomotives (#122) and cars (#123)
Compatibility	Because the motor and power supply are onboard in 4.5 V trains, they can be used on all track types.

Summary: Blue Era 12 V Electrified Rail System

Power	12 V transformer, center electric rail, 12 V train motor (#x550a)
Track	Blue single plastic rails, center electric rail, white crossties (2×8 plates)
Sets	Freight train with track (#725 and others)
Compatibility	Because the power comes from the electric rail, 12 V track must be used. 12 V trains from the Gray Era can also be used on 12 V track from the Blue Era.

THE GRAY ERA (1980–1990)

LEGO Trains entered a "golden age" in 1980 with the introduction of so-called Gray Era trains, named for their gray rails. The trains were more realistic and fit perfectly with the LEGOLAND theme of City sets. This era saw the introduction of accessories such as remote control switches and signals. The big steam engine (#7750), the remote control level crossing (#7866), and a number of other sets from this era enjoy cult status among collectors.

The color of the rails is not the only thing that's different about this era, though—the way the rails connect to the crossties differs, too. The familiar studs were replaced with clips that made track layouts much more stable and better suited for play.

The Gray Era sets remained in shops until the early 1990s, but no new sets were introduced after 1986, when the LEGO railway fell into its first hibernation.

POWER SOURCES

The Gray Era has unpowered trains and 4.5 V battery-powered trains, but the focus is clearly on the 12 V electrified rail system, with its many accessories. In this era, electricity is no longer used just to power trains—it also provides power for lights, control switches, signals, and even a powered level crossing.

The clips make the connection between rails and crossties more secure.

My first set from the Gray Era (#7740)

4.5 V BATTERY-POWERED SYSTEM

The 4.5 V trains are powered by three C batteries carried in a special battery car. Only two 4.5 V sets were released (#7720 and #7722).

12 V ELECTRIFIED RAIL SYSTEM

The Gray Era 12 V system brings many improvements over the Blue Era. While the Gray Era transformer is a little less powerful than its predecessor, the remote controls for signals and switches can be plugged directly into the side of the control unit.

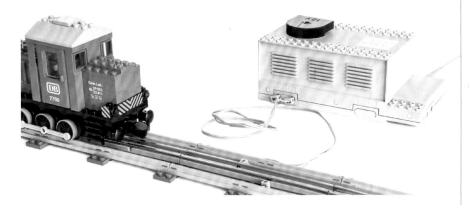

Gray Era transformer

The Gray Era 12 V motor is more compact than its predecessor and fits underneath a train baseplate. With its pin on top, it can be used as a truck. The wheels are fixed to the two driving axles. A third wheel can be connected on either side, finally allowing for three-axle trucks. The electrical contacts are integrated into the motor housing base, and a cable can be plugged in on top to connect lights.

Gray Era 12 V train motor

Straight 12 V track from the Gray Era

Curved 12 V track from the Gray Era

Gray Era switch

TRACKS

Rails are light gray and crossties are dark gray, a color scheme that makes the track look less like a toy than the blue and white of the previous era.

STRAIGHT TRACK

Straight track in the Gray Era is still made up of individual 16-stud-long (5 inch) rails. To convert to 12 V, simply add the electric rails (#7854).

CURVED TRACK

Curved track (#7851) has a shorter inside rail with a smooth surface and a longer outside rail with a ribbed surface. Its geometry matches the curved track segments of the Blue Era.

SWITCHES

Switches for LEGO railways are produced in left-handed or right-handed versions. Like the Blue Era, the Gray Era has hand-operated switches for 4.5 V (#7852), hand-operated switches for 12 V (#7856), and remote-controlled switches for 12 V (#7858 and #7859). The hand-operated 12 V switches can be converted to remote control with set #7863.

The two parallel tracks are close together and thus suffer from the same pitfalls as the switches from the Blue Era, so collisions of "wide" trains are very possible. The switches nonetheless allow compact designs, passing loops, multilevel sidings, and similar tricks.

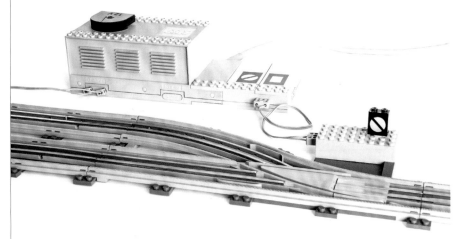

CROSSINGS

A crossing is available for 4.5 V (#7853) and 12 V (#7857).

12 V crossing from the Gray Era

REMOTE-CONTROLLED ACCESSORIES

The popularity of the Gray Era today is mostly thanks to the range of remote-controlled accessories, which contain a number of clever and unique features in an elegant design. Remote-controlled units can be connected to the gray transformer to extend control beyond just the running of the trains, allowing for completely remote-controlled operation:

- Right (#7858) and left (#7859) switches.
- Signal (#7860) with red and green lights; if the signal is on red, power to the track is interrupted and the train stops.
- Level crossing (#7866) with barriers that open and close and a flashing red light.
- Decoupler (#7862) to automatically decouple two wagons; unfortunately, the mechanism is unreliable, to say the least.

On top of all that, there are lights (for example, #7867) that can be connected to the transformer.

Remote-controlled 12 V signal (#7860) from the Gray Era

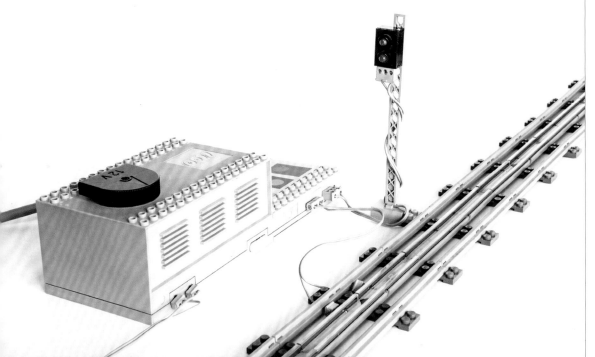

OTHER ELEMENTS

In the Gray Era, the LEGO designers seemed to have free rein and developed numerous special parts for trains.

WHEELS

Train wheels from the Gray Era

Gray Era train wheels, like the Blue Era wheels, are available in red and black. Besides the standard 0.65 inch size, a slightly larger wheel (0.94 inch tread, 1.14 inch flange) was produced only in red and used only in steam engine set #7750 and service packs #1143 and #5071.

The wheels are connected to a black 2×4 wheel holder brick and can be removed only with considerable force. These wheels perform slightly better than the Blue Era wheels, but I use them only as leading or trailing wheels.

Train motors also have wheels that can't be removed, with rubber bands for traction. The wheels have extra holes for clipping in connecting rods, which are used in some small steam and diesel engines.

Gray Era engine with connecting rods

BASEPLATE

A special baseplate is available for locomotives and wagons with trucks. It measures 6×28 studs and has holes for the pins on top of trucks and for feeding cables through.

TRUCKS

Typical truck from the Gray Era

Trucks are often used in combination with the new train baseplate. An important part is the train bogie plate. From below, it looks like a regular 4×6 plate, but the top is smooth and has a pin in the middle, which allows the train to articulate.

COUPLINGS AND BUFFERS

In the Gray Era, the red and blue coupling magnets are replaced by smaller black magnets, which can turn freely in their couplings. The coupling itself is clipped onto a new buffer beam, which can turn to go through curves.

Buffer beams with couplings from the Gray Era

WINDOWS AND DOORS

Naturally, LEGO minifigures want to enjoy a view of the passing landscape during their journey. Minifigures were introduced in the late 1970s, just before the beginning of the Gray Era, and influenced the design of the Gray Era train elements. The LEGO designers developed new train windows (1×4×3 and 1×2×3) and doors (1×4×5) to accommodate them.

LIGHT BRICKS

Working lights in locomotives are a real eye-catcher. Prisms placed inside special 1×6 bricks split the light from a 2×2 light brick into two beams for the headlights. This feature is included in some bigger sets (#7740, for example) and can be added to others with accessory set #7861.

Doors and windows from the Gray Era

WEIGHTED BRICKS

The weight of the 12 V train motor is not always sufficient for a locomotive to get traction on the tracks, so some locomotives have a special weighted brick included in the design.

12 V lights

SEEN FROM TODAY'S PERSPECTIVE

The Gray Era 12 V system will always have cult status. Well-maintained sets from this era are beloved—and expensive. For newcomers, current prices will be a deterrent, and a Gray Era 12 V railway will probably remain a dream. Then again, you might get lucky.

Not all parts have aged well, though. Motors are not meant to be opened, but there are many tutorials available on the internet that show how to reach the internals and carry out necessary repairs.

Weighted bricks

Summary: Gray Era 4.5 V Battery-Powered System

Power	Three 1.5 V (C) batteries in battery car, 4.5 V train motor
Track	Single plastic rails, crossties with clips (dark gray 2×8 plates)
Sets	Freight train (#7720 and others)
Compatibility	Because the motor and power supply are onboard in 4.5 V trains, they can be used on all track types.

Summary: Gray Era 12 V Electrified Rail System

Power	12 V transformer, center electric rail, 12 V train motor (#7865)
Track	Single plastic rails, powered metal rails, crossties with clips (dark gray 2×8 plates)
Sets	Many sets with cult status (#7750, #7740, #7866, and others)
Accessories	Level crossing with remote control barriers and flashing lights (#7866), remote control decoupler (#7862), remote control signal (#7860), remote control switches (#7858 and #7869), and lighting (#7861 and #7867)
Compatibility	The 12 V train motor from the Blue Era can be used on Gray Era track.

THE 9 VOLT ERA (1991–2005)

The 9 Volt Electric System was introduced in 1991, combining the Trains theme and LEGO's general-purpose 9 V system, which was introduced in the late 1980s.

Set #4551 from 1991

Gone are the days of LEGO trains with many remote-controlled functions. In this era, only the speed of the trains can be controlled from the relatively weak transformer, which is incapable of powering more than one train at a time. Critics of this era say that the locomotives and cars bear little resemblance to their real-life counterparts.

But around the year 2000, LEGO began to connect with its adult fans and developed a line of bigger and more detailed Exclusive sets for this newly discovered market.

POWER SUPPLIES

With the new system comes yet another power supply. The most notable feature of the general 9 V system is the Light and Sound system, introduced in 1986, which equips police and fire trucks with flashing lights and sirens. Later, the 9 V system expanded to include LEGO themes like Trains and Technic.

The 9 V system for trains is dominated by the train motor. Using 9 V cables and special 2×2 plates with contacts allows you to add lights to your train engines.

In 9 Volt Era track, the power is provided through metal rails, rather than a third electric rail. This looks much more realistic than the previous rail designs. The transformer looks like a phone charger and plugs into a wall outlet.

The train controller connects to the track with a special cable (#10078) and has one big yellow dial for controlling the speed of the trains.

Speed regulator

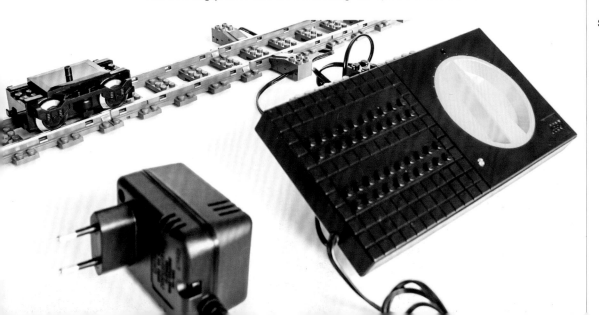

27

TRAIN MOTOR

At first sight, the 9 V train motor looks a lot like its 12 V predecessor: it has a black housing with fixed wheels and a pin in the middle. An obvious difference is the slightly bigger and shallower wheels. The wheels' metal flanges press against the metal rails with a spring and picks up the power for the motor. The wheels' treads have a rubber ring for grip.

The 9 V train motor

The pin in the middle can be used to turn the motor into a truck. There are also regular studs for connecting the decorative sides, as well as studs with metal patches for connecting a cable for the train lights.

The third axle of the 12 V motor is no longer included on the 9 V motor. Because of the bigger wheels, there is no room for a third wheel. There are little clips on the front and back of the motor housing. The clips can hold a brick or plate, which is very useful for decorating the motor, but they break easily.

TRACKS

The 9 V system maintains the track geometry of its predecessors, with the exception of the switch. Nevertheless, there is some innovation. For the first time, power is transferred directly through the rails. The track looks more realistic than its predecessors thanks to the new rail profile and the metal surface.

For the 9 V system, a single mold is used for rails and crossties. These all-in-one track sections were first made in dark gray and later, after the color change in 2003, in the new dark bluish gray.

9 V track with powered metal rails

To make setup and takedown easier, LEGO introduced a new connection. The first and last crosstie of each section is a 1×8 plate with special clips along the outside that connect to the next section.

STRAIGHT TRACK

Straight track is produced in complete segments with fixed rails (#4515). These segments are 16 studs (5 inches) long with crossties, still 2×8 plates, set two studs apart.

CURVED TRACK

Similarly, curved track is produced in complete segments (#4520).

SWITCHES

In the 9 Volt Era, only manually controlled switches were sold (#4531). The switch not only selects the desired route of the trains, it also electrically isolates the opposite route.

Perhaps just as importantly, the geometry of the switches changed. The branching track no longer runs right beside the main track.

Using a bigger S-curve increased the distance between the rails to eight studs. Unfortunately, this improvement isn't all that it seems—it's a major challenge to design trains that can navigate these S-curves.

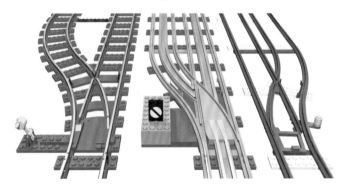

Switch geometries of three eras: 9 Volt Era, Gray Era, and Blue Era (from left to right)

CROSSINGS

The 9 Volt Era version of the crossing is set #4519.

OTHER ELEMENTS

The 9 Volt Era has few major innovations. Many of its parts—like buffer beams with magnets, the truck plates, and train baseplates from the previous era—remain in use, albeit with some minor changes.

WHEELS

Train wheels in the 9 Volt Era are completely different from those in previous eras—they look like real train wheels, and they behave like them, too. Train wheels from the 9 Volt Era have the lowest friction and are the best choice for train models. The wheels come only in black, but the wheel holders are available in old and new light gray as well as black. There are two slightly different versions. The older wheel can be used without the wheel holder because it has a tighter connection on the axle. These axles can be mounted in Technic pins (with a little play).

Beside these standard wheels with a 0.65 inch diameter (0.9 inch at the flange), there are also very small train wheels that connect to a 1×4 plate with wheel holder pins.

9 Volt Era train wheels, including small wheels (far left)

PANTOGRAPH

Pantograph (older version with smooth hinges)

A *pantograph* carries current from overhead wires to power a train. In the Gray Era, pantographs were built from regular LEGO parts, but the 9 Volt Era introduced a special pantograph shoe element. The first version fits in with the two- and three-finger hinge system of the time. When hinges changed to the click system in 2003, the pantograph part evolved to that new standard.

SINGLE-PURPOSE ELEMENTS

In the 1990s and 2000s, LEGO started producing more and more highly specialized parts as well as parts that could have been constructed out of other pieces. These parts are not particularly popular among LEGO fans, as they go against the spirit of creativity and free-form building.

The Trains theme did not escape this trend. Though some builders are able to make use of specialized "Train Front" elements, I prefer the challenge of modeling an aerodynamic shape with standard bricks and slopes.

SEEN FROM TODAY'S PERSPECTIVE

The rails and train wheels from the 9 Volt Era look good and are functional. Apart from the removal of the metal cover and some minor tweaks to the wheels, the modern Power Functions system uses the same components.

Compared to its predecessors, the 9 V train motor is not very robust. Repairs are officially not possible, but as with previous motors, tutorials are available for accessing their internals. For those who don't want to give up on the metal track, it is possible to transplant the electric motor from a Power Functions train motor into a 9 V train motor housing, but this operation involves a scalpel and soldering iron and isn't for the faint of heart.

For newcomers, the question is whether the investment in a 9 V LEGO railway is worth it. The price of straight track, switches, and train motors is now higher than the original retail price, sometimes double or more. The alternative is getting started with the Power Functions system. The 9 Volt Era track is compatible with that system, and 9 V trains can usually be converted to Power Functions—as long as there is room for a battery box and a receiver.

Dedicated train parts

Summary: 9 Volt Era System

Power	9 V controller, powered metal rails, 9 V train motor (#5300, #10153; these train motors have metal wheels to pick up the power from the rails)
Track	Powered track segments (9 V track)
Sets	Metroliner (#4558), Santa Fe Super Chief (#10020), Hobby Train (#10183), and many others
Compatibility	The 12 V train motors from the Blue and Gray Eras *cannot* be used with 9 V track.

LISTENING TO THEIR FANS

Realizing they had an asset in the LEGO community, the LEGO Group began interacting with its biggest fans, and the first LEGO Train Summit was held in New York in February 2001. Nine well-connected fans from all over the United States met with LEGO representatives to discuss their wishes and questions.

The LEGO Group responded to some of the suggestions, and suddenly train doors and windows were available in the LEGO online shop. The new My Own Train range included individual cars and a number of small steam engines in various colors. These sets were welcomed by LEGO train fans, both for inspiration and as a new source of parts.

Best of all, from this meeting came a few very detailed sets based on American prototypes like the famous Santa Fe Super Chief (#10020) with matching cars (#10022 and #10025). American LEGO fan James Mathis's work on these sets inspired a new generation of builders. The toy train suddenly turned into a model railway again.

But that wasn't the LEGO Group's only collaboration with train fans. The Hobby Train set (#10183), a universal train set released in 2007, marked the last set of the 9 Volt Era. It was developed with the help of a group of LEGO fans, including myself, who agreed on an inventory of standard parts and designed dozens of models based on them. After an internal review, we selected 30 of these models and produced digital building instructions to accompany the set.

The Hobby Train set (#10183)

32

Unfortunately, the models were developed so that they could be built with the 9 V train motor, based on the belief that the 9 V system would live on. But the release of the set was delayed by a year, and at that point the new RC system was already hitting the shelves. Due to budgeting, there are no motors or track in the Hobby Train set, and we had to grudgingly accept the replacement of dark green and dark red bricks with standard red.

The 9 V motor is visible in some of the box art, and a note had to be added on the box to warn buyers that no motor is included. The instruction booklet for the main model was so late coming back from the printer that it couldn't be put in the box and was supplied separately. Be warned: if you find a set #10183 in original packaging, that means there is no instruction manual included.

Despite these drawbacks, the Hobby Train set is a good "parts pack" for LEGO train fans, and you can find links to the building instructions in the Resources section at *www.nostarch.com/legotrains*.

THE RC ERA (2006)

Lackluster sales and financial trouble in 2003 forced the LEGO Group to take a critical look at its product range.* As a result, many niche themes disappeared as quickly as they had appeared. To the dismay of many fans, the colors light gray, dark gray, and brown were replaced with new shades, and the palette of colors and shapes was drastically reduced. The Make and Create theme, a forerunner of the current Creator theme, showed that LEGO was going back to its core business: creative models made from regular elements were back in style.

The LEGO Trains theme was hit by the cost-saving measures, and the 9 V system was axed. Production costs for the metal rails were deemed too high, so the metal had to go. The Power Functions system was only in the early stages of development and not yet market-ready. The Trains theme had to be

---

* For an account of the LEGO Group's corporate history, including its recovery from turmoil during this period, read David C. Robertson's *Brick by Brick* (Crown, 2013).

kept alive, so in 2006 the interim solution, the Remote Control system, was introduced with only two sets (#7897 and #7898).

POWER SUPPLIES

Despite being the same voltage, the new RC motor (#8866) cannot keep up with the old 9 V train motor. It no longer has fixed wheels; instead, it has new wheels that fit on 6-stud-long Technic axles. The tread has a rubber ring for improved grip like before, but it soon became clear that the ring is too slippery. Clever fans have replaced theirs with O-rings from plumbing supplies.

The RC train motor

Power comes from six AA batteries that fit inside the bulky new train base, which also houses the infrared receiver. The old 9 V cables are still used to connect the motor to the battery box. For the first time, trains are controlled by a handheld infrared remote control.

The bulky train base and the underpowered train motor found no favor with fans, who were glad to see this stopgap solution disappear.

TRACKS

In this era, a little plastic was added to the rails to compensate for the removed metal layer, keeping the height the same. Once again, the geometry did not change.

The crossing was dropped from the range and never replaced, but in 2007 LEGO surprised everyone with the release of set #7996, a double crossover that was the first new piece of track geometry. Barely a year later, the set disappeared from the range again, and it has since been sold for exorbitant prices

A true rarity: set #7996, a double crossover

on the secondhand market. The rarity of the piece remains a source of great lamentation for many LEGO train fans.

MAGNET COUPLINGS

The RC Era, brief as it was, came with only one notable new element. New laws meant the end of the old magnet couplings, which could be used in many different ways. The new magnet couplings cannot be removed from the buffer beam, which itself now comes in two versions: a standard one, and one with a snow plow. The old and new couplings are compatible; the new ones are just not as flexible a solution as the old ones.

The new (left) and old (right) magnet couplings

SEEN FROM TODAY'S PERSPECTIVE

Apart from the electrical components, the parts from the two sets in this brief era blend in with any LEGO collection. But the RC train motor does not really deserve that title, as it is just too weak to run a LEGO train. For that reason, the RC system is best avoided.

Summary: RC System

Power	Baseplate with integrated receiver and battery box, motor (#8866)
Track	Plastic track segments
Sets	Passenger train (#7897), Freight train (#7898)
Compatibility	With motor and power supply together onboard, the RC trains can run on all types of track.

REPLACING RUBBER WHEEL TREADS

The inner tube of a racing bicycle tire can be used as a cheap alternative to the rubber rings on train wheels. Cut it into thin slices, and it fits nicely around driving wheels from the Blue and Gray Eras.

O-rings from the plumbing department in hardware stores are also a suitable replacement for the rubber rings on RC Era trains. Look for rings that are 11/16 inch outside diameter × 9/16 inch inside diameter × 1/16 inch thick.

Bicycle inner tube used for train wheel traction

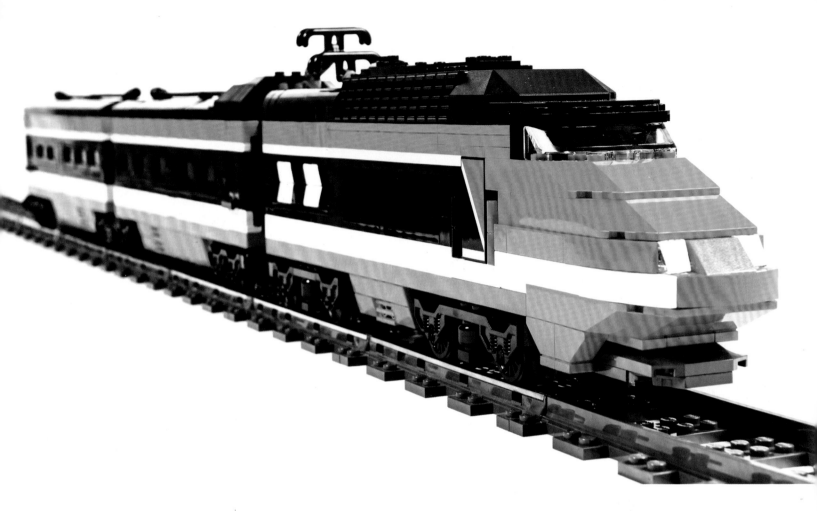

**Set #10223, Horizon Express
with Power Functions**

THE POWER FUNCTIONS ERA (2007–PRESENT)

In 2007, LEGO rolled out a new universal system for electric components in LEGO models across all themes, called Power Functions. The first set was the remote-controlled Technic bulldozer (#8275), and the first Power Functions train sets were Emerald Night (#10194) and the City theme Passenger Train (#7938) and Cargo Train (#7939).

There are many different components in the Power Functions system, most of which can be used for trains:

Motors

- Regular motors in sizes XL (#8882), L (#88003), and M (#8883)
- Train motor (#88002)
- Servo motor (#88004)

Batteries

- Battery box for six AA batteries (#8881)
- Battery box for six AAA batteries (#88000)
- Rechargeable battery box (#8878) with wall charger (#8887)

Controllers

- Remote control with speed control (#8879)
- Remote control without speed control (#8885)

Receivers

- Infrared receiver (#8884)
- Infrared receiver V2, used only in set #9398

Cables

- Extension cables in 8-inch (#8886) and 20-inch (#8871) lengths. One end is compatible with both Power Functions and old 9 Volt motors.

Miscellaneous

- Light set (#8870)
- Polarity switch (#8869)
- Linear actuators in two sizes (7–9 studs and 10–15 studs)

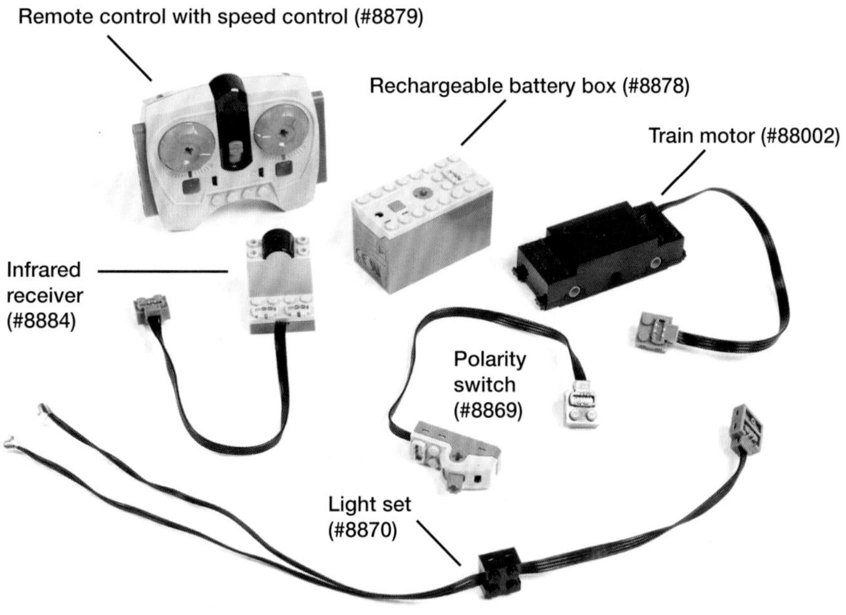

Remote control with speed control (#8879)

Rechargeable battery box (#8878)

Train motor (#88002)

Infrared receiver (#8884)

Polarity switch (#8869)

Light set (#8870)

Power Functions components for LEGO trains

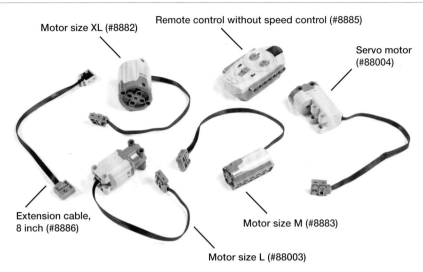

Motor size XL (#8882)

Remote control without speed control (#8885)

Servo motor (#88004)

Extension cable, 8 inch (#8886)

Motor size M (#8883)

Motor size L (#88003)

Unusually, the system uses four-core cables. The outer wires carry the power (9 V, 0 V), and the inner wires are for controlling elements like the motor speed. Lights and motors can also be connected directly to the power supply, but if you do so, you can no longer control the speed or brightness.

POWER SUPPLIES

The Power Functions system includes different options for driving locomotives, giving builders more possibilities for developing their own models.

POWER FUNCTIONS TRAIN MOTOR

The Power Functions train motor (#88002) is the obvious power solution. Identical in size and shape to the 9 Volt and RC train motors, it still has a pin for use as a truck and studs for building. The decorative side will cover the wheels; you'll need the version with cutouts for axles. You can see the decorative side and the Technic axle in the trucks on the Horizon Express on page 36.

The Power Functions train motor (#88002) is very recognizable with its bright orange axle holders.

Noticeably different is the fact that this motor has an attached cable for connecting it to the receiver. As with the RC train motor, there are no fixed wheels; instead, 6-long Technic axles are used. The axle holders are bright orange, a common feature in all Power Functions motors. Small wheels with Technic cross-holes and better rubber rings, available in black and red, complete this setup.

The motor housing is no longer hermetically closed like its predecessors. Instead, there are four T6 screws underneath that hold the two housing halves together.

French LEGO fan Philippe "Philo" Hurbain (*www.philohome.com*) has carried out extensive tests on all LEGO electrical components. His results show that the performance of the Power Functions train motor is better than that of its predecessors.

BUILD YOUR OWN DRIVETRAINS

Complex drivetrains can also be built with the standard Power Functions motors. The power from the motor is transferred to the wheels via Technic axles and gears. This allows for steam engines with driving wheels.

The Power Functions system opens up many new building opportunities for LEGO train builders. The new possibilities for building powerful drive configurations, and the ability to choose and optimize gear ratios to suit individual models, are welcome shifts in building methodology.

Power Functions drivetrain in the Swiss Be 6/8 "Crocodile," powered by an M motor

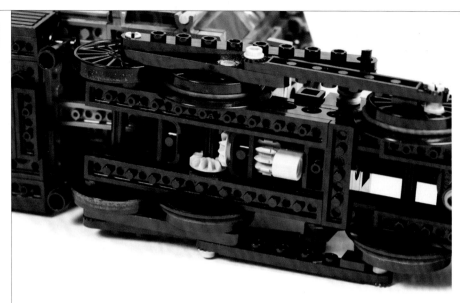

Power Functions drivetrain in the "Crocodile" (bottom view)

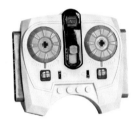

Power Functions remote control

CONTROL UNITS

The remote control unit with speed control (#8879) can control two trains on each of its four channels. The speed dials control the motor's speed in seven steps. The remote control itself uses three AAA batteries.

The control signals are sent to the receiver (#8884) by infrared light. That means the receiver must be placed in the train so that the remote control can have a line of sight to the curved "eye" at the top. The receiver is connected to the battery box with the attached cable.

The controlled devices, like motors and lights, are connected to the two outputs on the receiver.

BATTERY BOXES

There are two battery boxes that are suitable for use in a train: one that holds six AAA batteries (#88000) and one that is rechargeable (#8878). Both are 8 studs long, 4 studs wide, and 4 bricks tall, but they need a bit more space above to allow for the cable to be connected. It is often a challenge to find the room for the battery box when designing a locomotive.

The more expensive rechargeable battery has the advantage that it can remain in the model while it is charging. You must remove the AAA battery box from the train to change batteries.

Some LEGO Train builders have also successfully integrated the larger, more powerful AA battery box (#8881) traditionally used in Technic models.

TRACKS

The available track pieces in the Power Functions Era are the same as those in the RC Era. The only new component is the flexible track segment.

The idea for the flexible track was born during a Power Functions workshop held at LEGO headquarters in Billund, Denmark, where fans had been invited to consult with LEGO designers. LEGO seemed unwilling to develop track in different lengths or curve diameters, so the only remaining option was a flexible track segment. The inspiration came from the flexible elements of the Carrera Strax road system.

Flexible track

Although it was essentially a useful enhancement, unfortunately the LEGO Flex Track (#7499 and #8867) was not a commercial success. The main complaints were that it was too noisy, too prone to derailments, and too visually different from normal track.

WHEELS

The Power Functions system has the biggest range of train wheels. Most significantly, it includes train wheels with Technic cross-holes. There are also steam engine wheels, which are available in black and red and come with or without a flange. The wheel with a flange has a groove for a rubber band, which is necessary for traction. The diameter is 1.18 inches (1.46 inches at the flange), so a minimum of 4 studs is needed between the axles—3 if one of the wheels has no flange. These wheels have a Technic cross-hole in the middle, and connecting rods and piston rods can be connected by a pin hole at a 1-stud offset. Like many real steam engine wheels, they have a counterweight opposite the pin hole.

Power Functions Era train wheels

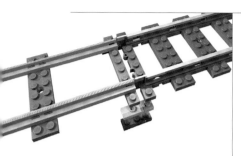

Transitioning from old to new track is no problem.

It looks like the universal Power Functions system will remain in the product range for another few years.

After my initial skepticism, I now unreservedly recommend the Power Functions system. With a little ingenuity, you can build a remote control for points, and the overall system is robust. The Power Functions train motor is particularly good, and the range of available motors gives builders more options than ever before. Finally, it is possible to build steam engines without moving the motor to the tender or a wagon.

The best way to get started with this system is by buying one of the big Power Functions train sets. In addition to the train, those sets include tracks and all the necessary Power Functions components. Older tracks from the Blue or Gray Eras can easily be combined with the current track segments, and because the Power Functions trains have a motor and battery onboard, they can run on every type of LEGO track.

Summary: Power Functions System

Power	Power Functions train motor (#88002) or other Power Functions motors with custom-built drivetrain, onboard battery box, and receiver
Track	Plastic track segments (RC track), Flex Track
Sets	Various regular and Exclusive sets like Emerald Night (#10194), Maersk Train (#10219), and Horizon Express (#10233)
Compatibility	With motor and power supply together onboard, the Power Functions trains can run on all types of track.

OTHER LEGO TRACK SYSTEMS

Besides the regular trains, there are some other track systems in LEGO's diverse range of themes: monorail and narrow gauge track.

MONORAIL

LEGO Monorail was introduced in 1987. Based on the 9 V system of the day, the special motor drives a gear underneath the train that grips the track like a cog railway. Powered by these motors, the short trains run their loops through urban or sci-fi landscapes.

These days, the Monorail is still hugely popular among LEGO fans, which is reflected in the prices on the secondhand market.

NARROW GAUGE TRACK

Some sets outside the Trains theme (for example #7199, #7065, and #6857) use narrow gauge track. Oddly, only curves and ramps have been produced, making these tracks look more like rollercoasters.

However, these track segments can be combined with single rails from the Blue or Gray Eras to create a working narrow gauge layout. It is even possible to create a custom narrow drivetrain with the Power Functions motors.

Narrow gauge track

CONCLUSION

For more than 50 years, the various LEGO train systems have attracted fans and collectors. Each era has its own charm, and you might favor the system you played with in your childhood. As a hobbyist, though, it's a good idea to know about the pros and cons of each system, the specific ways the trains are powered, and the elements that characterize each era.

This is where your creativity begins—there are no limits, and you can fit old Blue Era 2×2 windows alongside today's curved elements in your models. In the next chapter, we'll explore various LEGO elements and building techniques that will serve you well as you design your own trains.

BASIC PRINCIPLES

Let's dive into the world of LEGO elements and explore the endless ways to connect them.

It doesn't take much to start designing your own LEGO models, but it can feel challenging at first. It's like a three-dimensional puzzle where you only have so many pieces to use. Despite the limited "palette," however, there are nearly limitless ways of connecting pieces, and fans regularly find new, creative ways of doing so. The more familiar you become with the available pieces and building techniques, the easier it is to make your own creations.

BASIC LEGO PIECES

Let's start with the basics. At a general level, LEGO parts are available in the following categories: bricks, plates, slopes and wedges, tiles, bars, and wheels.

Bricks are the most common type of piece available to builders. They come in many varieties.

Bricks in various shapes

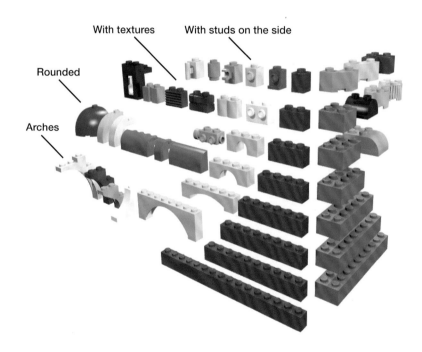

With textures

With studs on the side

Rounded

Arches

Plates are like bricks but not as tall. Three plates stacked on top of each other are the same height as a brick.

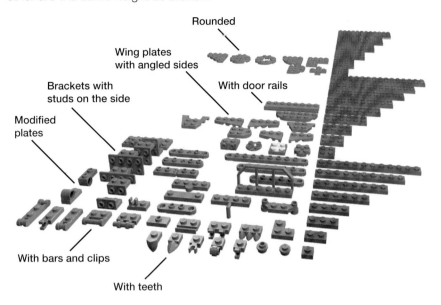

Rounded

Wing plates with angled sides

Brackets with studs on the side

With door rails

Modified plates

With bars and clips

With teeth

Slopes and wedges are bricks with one or more angled sides.

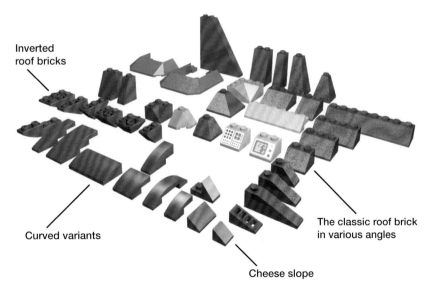

Inverted roof bricks

Curved variants

Cheese slope

The classic roof brick in various angles

Tiles are plates with a smooth surface.

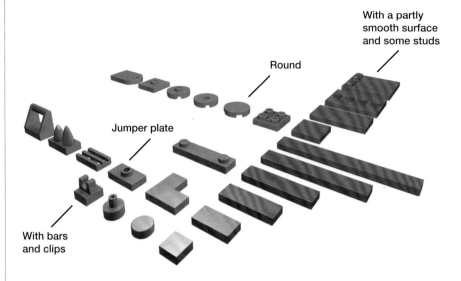

With a partly smooth surface and some studs

Round

Jumper plate

With bars and clips

Bars are elements that can be held by a minifig hand or a clip. The end of a bar may also be inserted in a hollow stud.

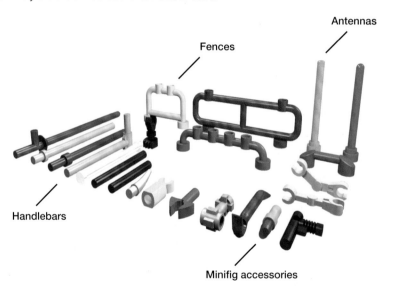

Antennas

Fences

Handlebars

Minifig accessories

Wheels come in many varieties, and as most LEGO fans know, LEGO is the world's biggest tire manufacturer!

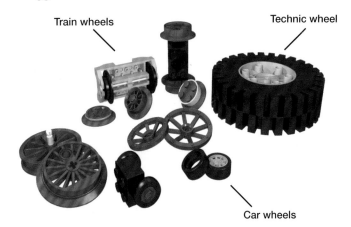

Train wheels

Technic wheel

Car wheels

Various wheels

When it comes to naming pieces, LEGO fans follow a certain convention. Calling a part "an eight" isn't clear; it could be a 1×8 or a 2×4, a brick or a plate. That's why LEGO fans are specific, calling a piece a "1×8 brick" or a "2×4 plate."

HOW DO LEGO ELEMENTS STAY CONNECTED?

Now that you've been introduced to the basic pieces and the naming conventions they follow, you might be wondering how they all connect. That seems like a simple question, but when you're building an engine or a working drivetrain, it's crucial to understand how everything holds together.

There are two types of connections that standard parts can make:

Studs and anti-studs   A *stud* is the small circular bump or knob on the surface of a LEGO piece. The stud's counterpart is the *anti-stud*, or the indentation that the stud fits into. Bricks, plates, and tiles all have anti-studs underneath.

Studs and anti-studs

Bars and clips   The release of the minifigure introduced a second method of interconnecting LEGO elements—using bars and clips. Many parts include a bar with a diameter that fits perfectly in minifigures' hands, like the tools they hold. Likewise, many parts have clips or openings (such as hollow studs) that can hold those bars. This way of connecting LEGO pieces gives you unlimited angles and offsets to break away from the "straight lines" of the typical LEGO set.

The designers at LEGO can only use these "legal" connections in sets. LEGO fans have more freedom and can use all sorts of "illegal" connections to add more details to models. Some of these techniques offer clever and interesting new possibilities for capturing details or for mounting parts that would otherwise be impossible to include. There are some disadvantages to using "illegal" connections, however. They are often not as strong as "legal" connections and, in some cases, can put excessive mechanical stress on some parts, potentially weakening or breaking them.

LEGO TECHNIC CONNECTIONS

Compared to the more common connections we've just discussed, the LEGO Technic theme seems like a different universe, especially with current sets full of beams rather than bricks. These so-called *studless* elements can be connected via pins. Some pins are designed to hold fast ("with friction"), while others are designed to move freely to allow for the creation of machines and mechanisms. Technic elements can also be connected via cross-holes and axles. The holes in Technic pieces are designed for pins or axles to fit through them, but they can also connect to studs.

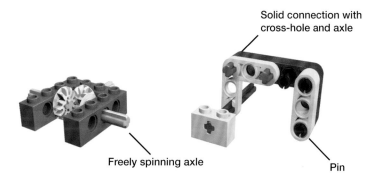

Solid connection with cross-hole and axle

Freely spinning axle

Pin

Movable and fixed connections using LEGO Technic parts

Technic elements allow for all sorts of creative reinforcements, which is important when you're building the housing for a powerful motor!

BUILDING TECHNIQUES

Whether it's a skyscraper, a sports car, or a train, when building a scale model, you'll be doing more than just stacking bricks. You'll need all sorts of complex constructions using various special parts.

When building a LEGO model train, you will face many challenges and will often need to make compromises. Usually, these compromises involve balancing several competing goals: having a powerful and reliable drivetrain, ensuring the model is robust and not overly delicate, maximizing detail in tight spaces, and making a model that can reliably navigate the tight geometry of LEGO track. Here are some tips from what I've learned in my own designs.

GEOMETRY OF LEGO BRICKS

LEGO bricks have a very specific geometry. A 1×1 LEGO brick has a 5:6 ratio of width to height. As mentioned earlier, a brick is as tall as a stack of three plates. And the height of a stack of five plates equals the width of a two-stud brick.

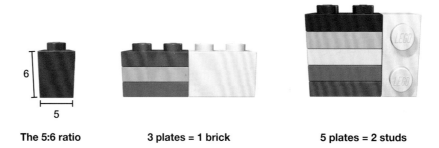

The 5:6 ratio   **3 plates = 1 brick**   **5 plates = 2 studs**

For example, that means a stack of five 1×2 plates is as tall as it is wide—in other words, it forms a square. You can use this trick to make a vertical stripe in a model or a row of books on a shelf.

Squares of 2×2 studs

A stack of five 1×6 bricks also creates a square.

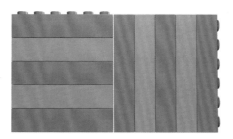

Squares of 6×6 studs

SNOT: BUILDING IN ALL DIRECTIONS

Studs not on top (SNOT) building techniques let you break away from the simple "brick on top of brick" geometry. Using this approach, you can attach parts or sections upside down or at an angle, make your models more detailed, and build in a smarter and more compact fashion. You can also simulate parts that don't exist. Here are some ways to use SNOT techniques.

THE HEADLIGHT BRICK

The headlight brick is the perfect all-purpose brick for LEGO model builders. It has a bit of a cult following, as is evident from its many nicknames. Its "official name" on BrickLink is "Brick, Modified 1×1 with Headlight" because of its original use (to give a car headlights), but you may also hear it called an Erling brick, after LEGO designer Erling Dideriksen, who created this element in 1979.

The geometry of this brick is very interesting. It has two studs, one on top and one on the side that is slightly inset. The brick also has two anti-studs, one underneath and one in the back.

If you turn the headlight brick so the side stud is facing up and put a plate on top, the combination is as tall as a brick. The top stud is now on the side and is flush, not inset, and can be used to attach other elements.

Headlight bricks in different positions. A headlight brick on its back with a plate on top is as tall as a standard brick (right).

The positions of the two studs make this a useful piece for SNOT building. For example, three plates fit neatly between two headlight bricks.

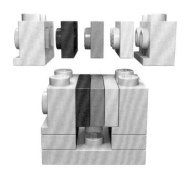

SNOT technique using headlight bricks

You can also create larger distances between the headlight bricks. Using what you learned earlier about the spacing of LEGO elements, you can add two studs between the headlight bricks, making room for five plates in the SNOT section.

You can create different distances between headlight bricks.

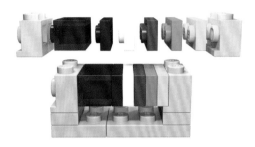

90° SNOT USING HEADLIGHT BRICKS

When you connect a tile to the inset stud of a headlight, it protrudes only a half-plate from the face of the brick, which allows for more subtle connections and decorative details.

90° SNOT using headlight bricks

180° SNOT USING HEADLIGHT BRICKS

Connecting two headlight bricks together allows you to connect a part or a section upside down.

180° SNOT using headlight bricks

90° SNOT USING BRICKS WITH STUDS ON THE SIDE

Besides the headlight brick, there's a whole array of LEGO bricks with studs on their sides. In the BrickLink catalog, you can find them in the "Brick, Modified" category.

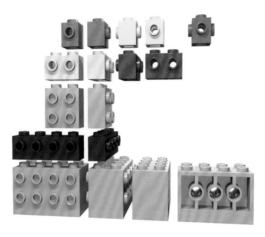

Bricks with studs on their sides

The 1×1 Technic brick and the 1×2 Technic brick with two holes are handy counterparts for the bricks with side studs thanks to the anti-studs formed by their axle holes. I often use them to connect plates when I create window frames (see "SNOT Technique for Train Windows" on page 56).

This technique can also be used to construct a 2-stud-wide SNOT section using five plates, as shown. And if you place two plates between two stacked bricks with side studs, the distance between the side studs is equal to a 3-stud-long plate. You can use this technique to connect larger sections sideways.

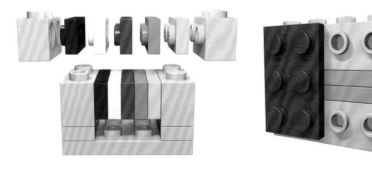

SNOT techniques using bricks with studs on the side

SNOT TECHNIQUE FOR TRAIN WINDOWS

There's a huge variety of window shapes and arrangements among railway rolling stock. Many of these window configurations can be represented with typical LEGO window parts, including window elements specifically designed for trains. However, you can better represent many window arrangements using SNOT techniques, in particular for modern passenger cars with long, narrow windows. Using SNOT also offers you more versatility since you can build window segments for nearly any length required.

I use the Technic bricks to form the vertical parts of the window frames (as mentioned earlier) and also to fill in gaps between the transparent panels.

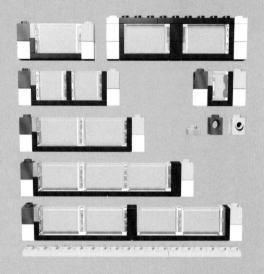

SNOT technique for modern train windows

90° SNOT USING PLATES, TILES, AND PANELS

You can make a 90° angle using only plates and tiles. The height or thickness of a plate (or of two thin panel walls) is exactly the same as the distance between two studs. This is not a very strong connection, so it lends itself mostly to decorative elements.

90° SNOT technique using panels, tiles, and plates

This is one of the oldest SNOT techniques, used in LEGO sets in the 1970s when special SNOT elements did not exist. It is now known as the *pony-ear technique*, after its use in set #697 to make the horses' ears.

90° SNOT USING BRACKETS

In recent years, the range of brackets has grown considerably. There are now brackets with side studs in 1×2, 1×4, 2×2, and 2×4 sizes. There are also "inverted" brackets where the thin side stands up.

90° SNOT technique using brackets

Many brackets have studs on top and on one side, but unlike the bricks described previously, the side studs sit on a thin plate. This plate is exactly half as thick as a normal plate, making brackets ideal for *microstriping*, discussed on page 64.

180° SNOT USING TECHNIC PLATES AND HINGES

The holes in Technic plates are meant for pins and axles, but since an axle hole can hold a stud, you can use a Technic plate to connect a part upside down.

180° SNOT technique using (old) Technic plates

If you turn one half of a pair of old hinge plates (also called *finger hinges*) around, you effectively create a 1×5 plate with two studs on either side, providing another way to connect an upside-down section. I've used this technique for the panels that hide the top of the driving wheels of the BR 10 steam engine.

180° SNOT technique using (old) finger hinge plates

Unfortunately, neither the Technic plates nor the hinge plates are in production anymore, but they can still be bought secondhand.

USING TILES TO FILL IN THE GAPS

When building sideways or upside down, you can end up with studs facing walls or other studs. In this case, tiles are your friend. They help you hide any ugly gaps in the SNOT section and leave a clean surface.

Tiles are useful when you use SNOT.

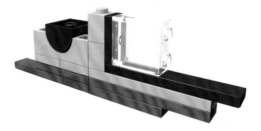

BUILDING OFF THE GRID

The spacing of the studs on LEGO bricks defines the grid that you normally build on. When you're looking to build more realistic models, this coarse grid is no longer sufficient, and you'll want to attach sections at an offset of less than one stud. For example, you might want to create a slightly recessed window while designing a building. Or, on a train model, you may need the offset for placing a gangway connection or coupling in just the right position.

To create such an offset, you can use special parts dedicated to that purpose, or you can connect basic parts in creative ways.

OFFSET IN ONE DIRECTION

The best-known and most important part for creating offsets is a 1×2 *jumper* plate with just a single stud in the middle of the top surface. This jumper plate gives a half-stud offset in one direction and is used, for example, to mount an odd-width assembly on an even-width base.

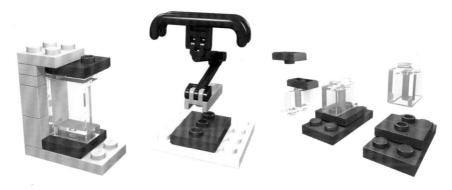

Offset using jumper plates

The 3×2 plate with a hole is useful as both an offset and a SNOT option.

Offset properties of the 3×2 plate with hole

There are two types of Technic bricks: those with holes between the studs and those with the holes directly below the studs. Combining the two types gives you a half-stud offset with a strong connection.

Stable offset connections using Technic bricks

Some parts have hollow studs, such as the "Plate, Round 2×2 with Rounded Bottom" (known as the *boat stud* because it makes it easy to slide a boat over a carpet). They present another way to create a half-stud offset: you can fit the small tubes on the underside of a 1-stud-wide piece into their hollow studs.

OFFSET IN TWO DIRECTIONS

When you need a half-stud offset in two directions, the obvious part to use is "Plate, Modified 2×2 with Groove and 1 Stud in Center," better known as the 2×2 jumper plate.

But long before this part was introduced in 2009, there were other ways to achieve the offset in two directions. For example, parts that are 2×2 or larger typically have hollow tubes underneath. In a normal construction, these tubes fit between the studs on another piece. But a stud can also fit inside the tube itself, creating an offset connection.

The 1×2 jumper plate can be used to make a similar connection: the hollow stud on top of the plate can hold the smaller tubes on the underside of single-width parts.

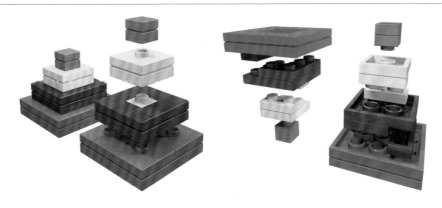

**Offset in two directions using the
2×2 jumper plate (yellow and blue)**

**Creating an offset in two directions by
attaching studs to the hollow tubes on
the underside of a plate**

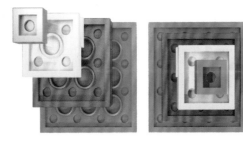

**Comparison of standard brick-on-brick connections
(left) and offset in two directions (right)**

**The stud from the jumper plate is attached
to the small tubes of the 1×3 brick.**

BUILDING IN ODD DIMENSIONS

Building with LEGO parts in odd dimensions has a special appeal, especially for train models. A width of seven studs is a good compromise between the extra detail of 8-wide trains and the performance of 6-wide trains on tight curves.

But building in an odd length also poses a challenge. First, there are not many bricks with odd dimensions. You can literally count the number of plates with an odd length on one hand: 1×1, 1×3, 2×3, and 3×3. Then there is the finicky business of connecting odd and even sections of your model.

The most important parts for me when building 7-stud-wide trains are the two 1×5 Technic plates, one with studs at the end and the other with holes at the end. They are the only 5-stud-long plates available, and they are wonderfully versatile. Because of the cross-hole in the middle, you can't just place them on top of other plates. But the open studs make them useful for offset builds, and you can use the ones with holes at the ends for upside-down SNOT building.

Elements with odd dimensions

Center cross-hole cannot connect to a stud.

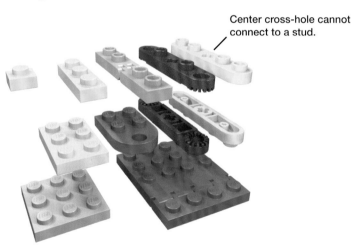

Building a 7-stud-wide base for a locomotive or wagon takes a lot more parts and creativity than building its 6- and 8-stud-wide cousins. Not only do you have to create an odd-width base from parts that mostly have even dimensions, but you also need to determine how and where to build the transition to an even section. One typical example would be the narrower ends of historical railway carriages.

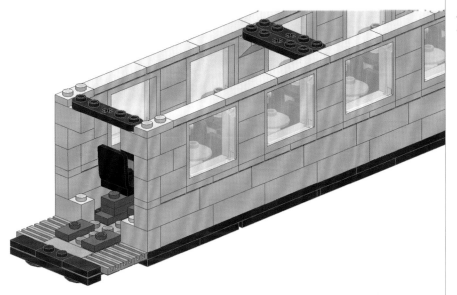

A 1×5 plate in action, used as a crossbar in this carriage

Longer train bases need pin holes to connect the trucks. The obvious candidates are the 3×2 plate with a hole on one side, or any Technic plate with a hole at the end. The longer the Technic plate is, the more studs it offers to connect to other elements of the train base. Depending on which part you use, the hole either aligns with a row of studs or sits between two rows.

Pin hole

Technic plates with holes at the ends are ideal for connecting train bases to trucks.

MICROSTRIPING

Microstriping means creating thin lines (typically half the height of a plate) using LEGO parts rather than stickers. A number of elements can be used for this purpose. Earlier in the chapter, we covered brackets that have their side studs on a panel that is half as thick as a normal plate, and these are perfect for the job. Other parts this size are the 2×2 flag and traffic signs.

The top of the 1×2 hinge brick is even thinner. When all you need is a simple line along a wall, you can use the 1×2 hinge brick. It is the same size as a normal brick, and you can swap the top part for a different color.

Another option is to use a flag or the thin side of a bracket to create a frame or border. The problem, of course, is that the rest of the element needs to be hidden inside the model. One solution is to put a plate and a tile on the sideways studs.

You can also use the microstriping technique as a means of bracing angled windows. For the angled windows of the upper deck of my bi-level car, I used transparent cheese slopes and transparent panels mounted with a SNOT technique.

I wanted to have a red border between the window and the gray roof, but there was very little room. The solution was the 1×2 – 2×4 bracket. The width of four studs matches the size of the window, and the 1×2 angled part lies far enough inside that it doesn't interfere with the window's appearance. The only problem is that minifigs will often hit their heads on the brackets.

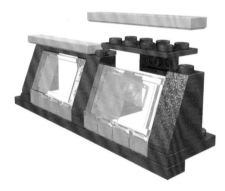

I also used light gray 1×2 – 2×2 brackets in the driver's cab. These continue the gray from the roof and frame the windshield and lights, while the outward-pointing studs hold the various curved pieces that form the stream-lined design of the cab.

Another 1×2 – 2×4 bracket fills the gap created by the SNOT-mounted tiles of the slightly recessed destination sign.

**The destination sign of the
Regional-Express is framed by
the thin edge of a bracket.**

TEXTURES

Modern passenger trains don't have a complex outer skin, but historical trains, freight wagons, and steam trains offer more variety, which can also be mod-olod in LEGO.

In reality, older trains rarely look brand new, so why not add some rust and graffiti to your LEGO models? Various shades of red and brown can mimic rust on the aging metal of the wagons. Using a round or angled plate here and there will also make the model appear used.

You can also add realism by being creative with the orientation of parts. Using the bottoms of various pieces opens a new world of shapes and textures you can add to models. Tiles and newer jumper plates have a little groove along their base, and stacking a few of them creates a fine grille texture.

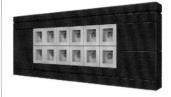

The bottom of 1×1 plates used as texture

Even plastic can get rusty.

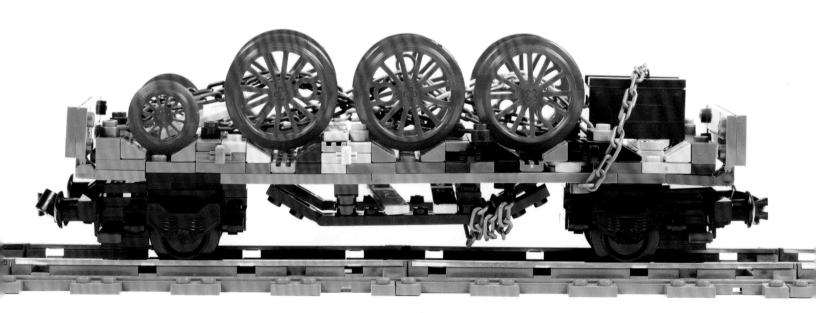

NICE PART USAGE!

The intended use of many specialized LEGO elements is obvious—for example, the palm trunk element creates a recognizable palm tree, and the ice skates clearly belong under minifigure feet. But these specialized parts can also be used in creative and unexpected ways. LEGO fans call this creative repurposing *NPU*, for *nice part usage*.

An ice skate used as a door handle

A palm tree trunk piece used as a smokestack

Even if you don't like weapons, it might be worth your while to check the "Minifig Weapon" category on BrickLink every now and then. Combined with a pair of binoculars and a few other pieces, the sheriff's revolver makes a pretty good pantograph!

Guns and binoculars used in a pantograph

A crowbar used as a brake lever

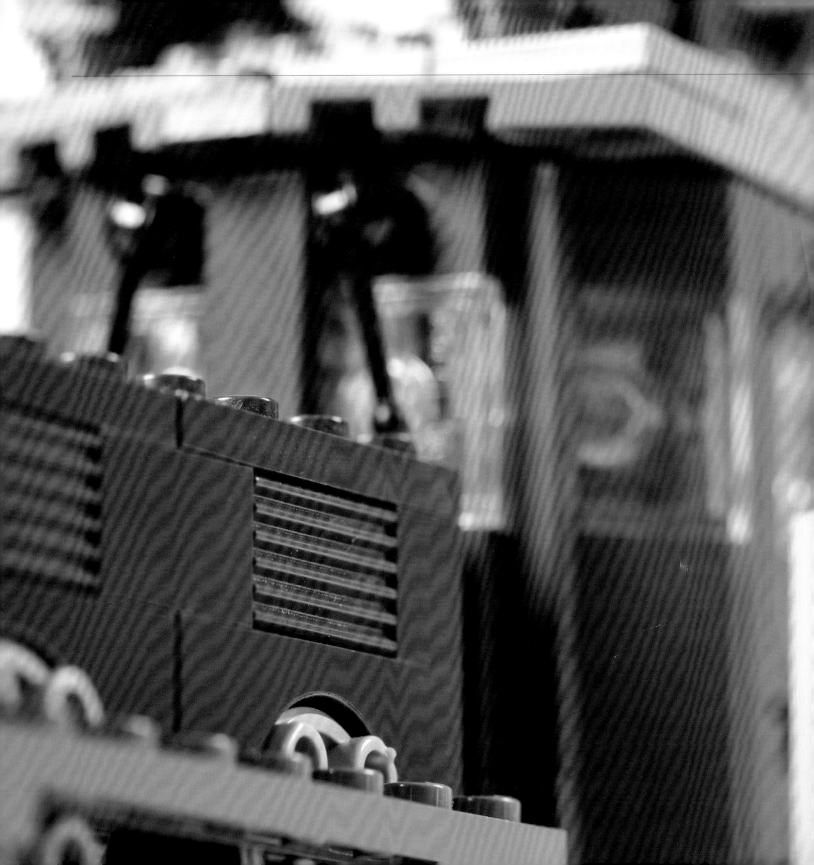

DESIGNING YOUR OWN MODELS

You might be wondering if you're ready to begin making your own models. Which train should you build? Maybe you should start with the commuter train that takes you to work every day, or a freight train? And who hasn't dreamed of a beautiful steam engine in LEGO?

Even if it seems impossible at first, you can develop LEGO trains into "proper" model railways to rival any traditional store-bought model train kit. Every year, fans create ever-more-detailed models, far beyond the trains you can find in official LEGO train sets.

This chapter explores the possibilities. Once you have an idea, you need to make a plan to convert it into LEGO. You'll face the challenges of designing to scale, powering your trains, and achieving a recognizable end result.

Once you've been building with LEGO for a while, it gets easier. You'll become familiar with the shapes and colors available to you, and you'll begin to see LEGO elements in some of your favorite trains.

CHOOSING A SCALE

Scale is everything for many modelers. Architects build models in exactly 1:100 or 1:50 scale in wood and cardboard. Traditional model railway builders live in their own universe, with scales called O (1:48), HO (1:87), or N (1:160). These devoted hobbyists argue over the size and position of every handrail and rivet to such an extent that they've earned the nickname *rivet counters*.

My model of the legendary Be 6/8 "Crocodile"

LEGO train modelers are different, as they have no official standards to work from. That said, there are several common approaches you might want to explore: minifig scale, L-gauge scale, and working backward from a recognizable LEGO element (most commonly a train wheel).

Building a recognizable model isn't about scaling every part exactly, although proportion matters. Intentionally omitting some details or exaggerating others is usually necessary. Scale modeling with LEGO is a bit like drawing a caricature: the end result may not be an exact likeness, but it is recognizable and undeniable.

MINIFIG SCALE

The LEGO Group owes a lot of its success to the minifigure. It's no surprise, then, that many LEGO fans use the minifigure as a reference for the size of their buildings and vehicles—including, of course, trains.

Putting a number to minifig scale is not easy, as the proportions of a minifig defy human anatomy. Compared to humans, minifigs are stocky, with short arms and legs and a very wide torso. Based purely on their height, minifig scale would be somewhere between 1:42 and 1:48.

L-GAUGE SCALE

You can also base your scale on the width or gauge of the LEGO track. This is known as *L-gauge* scale. LEGO track has a gauge of five studs (1.48 inches; 37.5 millimeters) when measured between the insides of the rails. That places L-gauge scale between the established 1 and O gauges.

Minifig proportions are somewhat exaggerated.

L-Gauge Compared to Traditional Model Railway Scales

	Original	1	L	O	HO
Standard gauge (mm)	1435	45	37.5	32	16.5
Standard gauge (in)	56.5	1.77	1.48	1.26	0.65
Scale	1:1	1:32	1:38	1:48	1:87

Canadian LEGO train builder Michael Gale (*www.l-gauge.org*) is putting a lot of effort into standardizing L-gauge as a means for LEGO fans to collaborate with one another.

LEGO track gauge

Taking the scale from the track gauge dictates the length and width. Consider the ICE 3 high-speed train, for example (a photo is shown on page 134).

An 81-foot ICE 3 car in 1:38 scale would measure an impressive 81 studs long (2 feet, 1 inch; 65 centimeters), and would be nearly 10 studs wide. At that scale, a full eight-car ICE 3 train would be over 16 feet long and would not fit on most LEGO train layouts. My own ICE 3 model is "only" 11 feet, 4 inches long and is already much too big for most track layouts.

SCALING BY WHEEL SIZE

A third scaling option is to work backward from a recognizable LEGO part. Since you'll be limited to certain wheels (see "A History of LEGO Trains" on page 9 for coverage of available wheels from each era), using a wheel-based scale is a good idea, especially when you're building a steam engine. Side views of real trains (in photo or blueprint form) are readily accessible online. Freely available image programs can easily scale the image so the wheels in the picture match the size of one of the available LEGO train wheels. When you print the picture, you'll have an idea of how big the engine should be.

Scaling using wheel size by overlaying images of LEGO wheels on an image of a real-life train

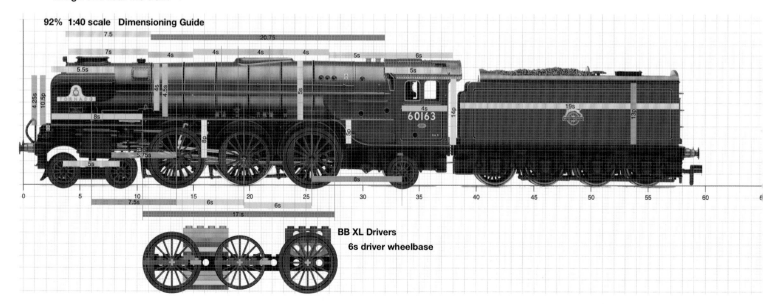

6-WIDE, 7-WIDE, 8-WIDE . . . OR MORE?

LEGO train models, especially cars, are typically shorter, to scale, than their full-size counterparts. But the length of a model isn't as important as the width for making it recognizable.

Based on the 1:38 scale for L-gauge, the trains should be 9 or 10 studs wide. For a static model, 9 or 10 studs is a fine choice, but it's not suitable for a model that needs to run on rails, because it makes for a heavy train that is difficult to operate.

Over time, you'll find the width that suits you. I started out building 8-wide models, but these days I prefer 7-wide.

6-, 7-, and 8-wide trains compared

6-WIDE: OFFICIAL LEGO TRAIN SCALE

The standard width for all official LEGO train sets is six studs. Locomotives and cars are as wide as the track and relatively short (in length) and tall (in height).

You don't need as many parts while working on 6-wide designs, and the train motor will have no problems pulling the train around the track. Tight curves and switches will not cause any issues.

The challenge with 6-wide trains is designing them to look more like a model than a toy. How do you get the characteristic details to fit in only six studs?

The LEGO sets in the Exclusive series, such as Santa Fe Super Chief (#10020), Maersk Container Train (#10219), and Horizon Express (#10233) are a good reference point. Steam engines in 6-wide are difficult because the cylinders, connecting rods, and piston rods lie outside the wheels. The proportions will look much better if the whole model is wider than six studs. LEGO designers achieved this with Emerald Night (#10194).

If you use the old blue or gray track, it's best to build trains in 6-wide. Because of the distance between parallel tracks (dictated by the switches), only 6-wide trains can pass each other safely.

7-WIDE: A REALISTIC-LOOKING SCALE

If you're up for a challenge and you want a realistic-looking train model, building in 7-wide might be right for you. An extra stud in width makes a big difference. Building the train base seven studs wide means that trucks and driving gears are slightly hidden beneath the main body, which is much more realistic. At this width, there is room to build your own trucks and hide the train wheels behind springs and stabilizers. A 7-wide train is a natural fit in the LEGO City scale, as well as with the Modular Buildings popularized by the Cafe Corner (#10182).

Building in 7-wide comes at a price, however. These models require many more parts than 6-wide designs, and they also require more complex building techniques. Seven is an odd number that doesn't fit well with most LEGO elements, which commonly have even dimensions. A 6-wide train can be built on 6-wide plates, but with a 7-wide train, you'll need a combination of plates with 3 + 4 or 6 + 1 studs. When you build LEGO models in odd widths, you'll learn to appreciate the few elements with odd dimensions (see "Building in Odd Dimensions" on page 62).

Not everything in a 7-wide model has an odd width, though. The trucks or the chassis between the wheels will have to be 6-wide to fit on the track. Of course, you'll have to use more parts to make the transition between the 7-wide body and its 6-wide trucks.

Building a train base with holes in the middle (so you can fit the pins on the trucks) is easy using the 3×2 plate with a hole (or the Technic plates with holes at the ends). You could also use a standard train base and then add brackets and tiles to widen it to just over 7 studs. That way, you don't have to worry about attaching trucks.

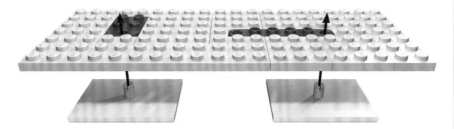

You'll have to get creative when building a 7-wide train base.

When you use more parts, the train will be heavier. But it's not that bad with a 7-wide train, and you can just add a second train motor to increase the pulling power.

The greater width allows for longer trains. A 7-wide car on trucks is usually between 40 and 50 studs long—a good compromise between scale model looks and tight curve performance.

Longer trains will likely have overhang issues. Along curves and through switches, sections of many train cars will protrude well beyond the edge of the track. This not only looks unrealistic, but it also risks collision with buildings and other lineside features close to the track. For example, the little yellow levers that control switches are notorious for interfering with passing trains. Luckily, you can change the switches without the yellow levers.

8-WIDE: A SCALE FOR DETAIL

LEGO train models built to a nominal 8-wide scale can achieve better scale fidelity than 7-wide. You can model many details on the train and around the trucks with the available space.

The extra width has a corresponding disadvantage: extra length. Rolling stock is typically at least 50 studs long. Despite the extra length, 7-wide and 8-wide trains have the same number of axles, so each axle on an 8-wide train holds more weight. LEGO train motors struggle to move all this weight at a reasonable speed, especially around curves and through switches. The overhang problem is even worse for 8-wide trains than it is for 7-wide trains.

Normal train wheels look small on 8-wide trains. A 50-stud-long locomotive may look impressive, but the relatively small wheels on the trucks spoil the overall impression of the model due to their disproportional scale. Using the larger spoked wheels from steam trains is not a convincing solution.

When building an 8-wide train, you can include many details without resorting to complex building techniques. Don't expect your train to run trouble-free around your layout, though, and don't expect it to fit on your friend's layout at the next exhibition.

CHOOSE YOUR OWN SCALE

LEGO trains have probably been built in every possible size and scale. If the model is built for display and doesn't need to run on track, then the sky's the limit. Inspiration for working in 1:20 scale (or "Miniland scale") can be found in the LEGOLAND theme parks. Microscale models present a fun challenge, too.

Very recognizable microscale trains by James Mathis

DESIGNING TO RUN ON TRACK

LEGO trains' toy-like character stands out when they take on tight curves. Even streetcars, squeaking their way through city streets, run on more comfortable curves. The tight curves of LEGO track are designed to fit on a bedroom floor, and building to that geometry requires creative solutions.

Having a short test track with switches and curves is essential when you're building a LEGO train model. Throughout the development, make sure the train can navigate the test track's curves and switches.

A locomotive or wagon that uses two sets of two-axle trucks is relatively easy. You can use standard building techniques that you find in LEGO sets, and you can focus all your attention on the design of the train's body.

A long-wheelbase, two-axle freight car is difficult to manage, but the most complex challenge is building a steam engine. Depending on the locomotive, it will have numerous axles, large and small wheels, and external driving gears that often make negotiating tight curves difficult. This challenge, however, hasn't stopped LEGO train builders around the world from designing steam engines. Builders continue to innovate solutions and techniques that produce locomotives capable of elegantly navigating their way through the unforgiving geometry of LEGO track.

While LEGO elements all fit together, it's not always easy to change a model from one track or propulsion system to another, so it's important to make a decision early on and stick with it. Wheel and axle configurations on the chassis or trucks can vary from train to train. For locomotives, two systems describe the wheel configuration (see "An Aside on Wheel Notation" on the next page).

Luckily, real trains don't encounter curves like these.

AN ASIDE ON WHEEL NOTATION

Locomotives are classified by their wheel arrangement. There are two main systems in use: the Whyte notation is used in the United States and United Kingdom, while the German VDEV/VMEV/UIC classification is more common in the rest of Europe.

Both systems describe groups of wheels or axles. The Whyte notation simply counts the number of wheels in each group. For example, the BR 10 would be a 4-6-2, meaning four wheels on the leading truck, followed by six driving wheels and two wheels on the trailing axle. A lot of wheel configurations have been given informal names, usually after the first locomotive that used it. A 4-6-2 layout is called a *Pacific*. The UIC classification is a bit more complex and denotes more details. In this classification, the BR 10 is a 2'C1', where the 2 means two axles and the prime symbol means they are connected to a truck, C means three driving axles on the main chassis, and 1' means a single trailing axle on a truck.

The UIC classification is also used for diesel and electric locomotives, while the Whyte notation covers only steam engines. For diesel and electric, the United Kingdom uses the UIC classification, while the United States uses the AAR wheel arrangement system, which is a simplified version of the UIC classification. For example, the Vectron in UIC terms is a Bo'Bo', with the primes meaning two trucks, each with two driving axles, and the *o* meaning that each axle has its own motor. In AAR, the Vectron would be a B-B, which again means two trucks with two driving axles each.

The Swiss Crocodile (see page 186 for building instructions) is a (1'C)(C1'), with the parentheses meaning that this locomotive has two chassis, each with three driving axles, and a single leading/trailing axle. In AAR notation, this would be a 1-C+C-1, with the + meaning two coupled chassis.

MIMICKING REAL-WORLD AXLES AND TRUCKS

Nowadays, rail vehicles with two axles are rare. Most locomotives and wagons have four axles. A long wagon with four fixed axles wouldn't be able to navigate curves, so the axles need to pivot, or "articulate." The common solution is to mount them in pairs in trucks or bogies (subframes that can pivot relative to the main chassis). The vast majority of locomotives and wagons have two trucks, but the number of axles can vary.

The wheels and type of drivetrain determine how the chassis or trucks are built. For example, when you use the train motor, you have little room left to design your own trucks. Sometimes the requirements of the prototype and the possibilities of a LEGO model are at odds (for example, when you want to build a three-axle truck using the regular train motor).

FIXED AXLES

If a train has to go around curves and through switches, fixed axles limit the length of a wagon or locomotive. Official LEGO designs typically limit cars with two fixed axles to six studs between the wheel holders. I recommend a maximum of 11 studs between axles. At that length, you'll notice a resistance going through the curves and the motor will have to work hard.

Basic car with fixed axles

A longer distance between axles is possible only when at least one axle isn't fixed. You can center the articulating axle with a few tricks—for example, using rubber bands (like the blue one shown here) or flexible hose—so that it looks like a fixed axle but can pivot a little when required.

Two-axle freight wagon with an articulating axle

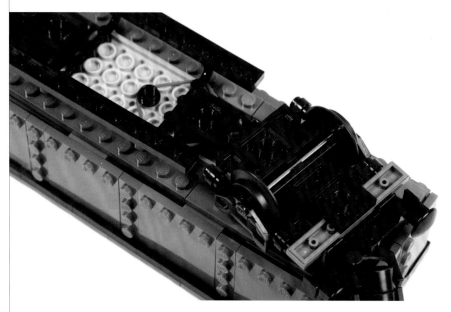

TRUCKS

A *truck* is a subframe with two, three, or four fixed axles. Two trucks are connected to the train base by a pin, around which the truck can turn.

Basic car with trucks

Trucks with two axles are easy to build. LEGO often makes the trucks with two side-by-side wheel holders, which is very compact. For locomotives, three studs between wheel sets are usually used to match the size of the train motor. If trucks are too long, performance through curves and switches will suffer.

Trucks with three axles are hard to build. A truck with three fixed axles can't navigate tight curves. A truck with a middle axle that can slide left and right might take tight curves well. The flanges on the wheels force the sliding axle back to the center when on straight track. Also, you can build the first or last axle as a pivoting leading or trailing axle—a technique typically used when the truck includes a train motor.

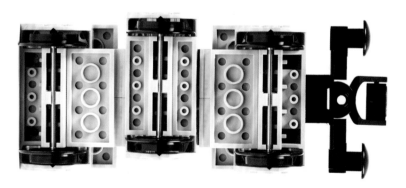

Three-axle truck with sliding middle axle on curved track

Three-axle truck with sliding middle axle, as seen from below

CONNECTING TRUCKS TO THE TRAIN BASE

You can easily attach trucks with a 4×6 train bogie plate. The pin on that plate has enough play to accommodate some uneven track connections—for example, where the track crosses the edge of two tables or at the start or end of an incline.

Another option is a 2×2 turntable plate or a Technic pin. In situations where a motor in the main body powers wheels in a truck, the axle that is part of the drivetrain fills the role of the truck's pivot pin.

JACOBS TRUCKS

Jacobs trucks (or *articulated bogies*) are a special type of truck shared between two cars. Jacobs trucks are usually used in streetcars, but the French TGV High Speed Train and intermodal container cars use them, too. Sharing trucks means fewer wheels and axles, resulting in more economical running.

The challenge with Jacobs trucks in LEGO is choosing pivot points that keep the cars as close together as possible without touching on curves.

Jacobs trucks

COUPLINGS AND BUFFERS

The movement of locomotives and cars relative to each other is possible because the couplings, usually mounted at the end of the car body, can rotate. In the real world, that rotation is only a few degrees, which is slight enough that you can walk between cars even when the train is going around a bend.

Couplings attached to the train base are possible only for short wagons.

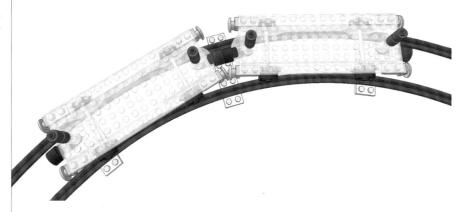

Buffer beam with coupling and buffers attached to the trucks

In Europe, the coupling is usually a chain with buffers placed on either side of the coupling on the buffer beam. These buffers help reduce slack in the coupling and reduce shocks during switching. Modern multiple units like high-speed trains have fixed couplings and don't need buffers. North American trains use automatic couplings and don't have buffers.

The tight curves of LEGO track require a thoughtful approach to attaching couplings and buffers on the model. Couplings and buffers cannot be attached to the train base of an engine or wagon, but instead have to be attached to the trucks. As a result, other details like steps for passengers and the buffer beam also need to be attached to the trucks, regardless of where they might be placed in the original train.

The combined pivot points of the truck and the magnet coupling allow enough rotation for your model to make it through curves and switches.

Standard pivot points for couplings and the resulting large distance between wagons

An additional pivot point for the couplers allows a tighter distance between wagons.

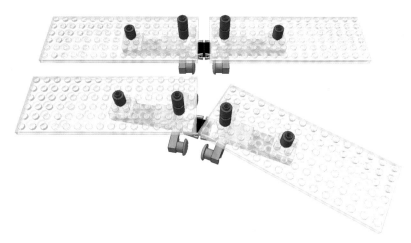

The pivot point of a truck does not necessarily have to be in the middle. For an even shorter coupling distance, you can move the pivot point of the truck, for example, by using the 2×2 turntable. Using a 2×2 turntable as a pivot point gives you more placement options than the classic 4×6 bogie plate does.

Try positioning the 2×2 turntable at either the first or second axle of your truck, and see how the pivoting action compares to the bogie plate.

Tho offoct of different pivot points for trucks

Through trial and error, I determine the best pivot points for the trucks and couplings for each model I build. As a rule, I look for the shortest coupling distance that still allows enough space between wagons on curves. Moving the truck pivot farther from the end of the train base means a shorter coupling distance but also creates more overhang on curves.

The same applies for the pivot point of the leading and trailing axles on steam engines, where it often works best to have the pivot point close to the nearest fixed axle.

LEGO's magnet couplings are typically strong enough to hold trains together. Only for very long, heavy trains do you need a stronger solution, such as using neodymium disc magnets between the LEGO magnets, or replacing the magnets altogether. The distance between the pins of two coupled magnets is five studs, so the magnet coupling can be replaced by a 5-stud-long Technic plate or liftarm. Another alternative is using ball-and-socket connections.

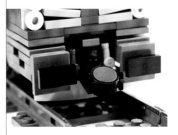

Magnet coupling and buffers on the Vectron locomotive

Depending on the size of the train model, there are different parts you can use to create buffers. The standard LEGO buffers (on buffer beams, or as single parts like they were in the 1970s) work fine for 6- or 7-wide trains but look a bit lost on larger models. Popular parts for homemade buffers include tiles and boat studs (Plate, Round 2×2 with Rounded Bottom).

BUILDING A STEAM ENGINE

The biggest challenge in fitting a LEGO train on a track is building a working model of a big steam engine or a historical engine like the Crocodile. The large driving wheels (also known as *main drivers*) are attached to a chassis and are linked with connecting rods and piston rods. When three or more axles with large wheels are fixed to a chassis, the train can't go around curves. You also need to consider leading and trailing axles. They improve drivability on real-life trains, but they can be a problem on LEGO models.

Here are some tips for building these complex locomotives in LEGO:

- Use wheels without a flange ("blind drivers").
- Use wheels that can slide sideways.
- Divide the driving wheels into smaller, pivoted units.
- Use connecting rods that are not connected to all wheels.
- Strategically place pivot points for leading and trailing axles.

The first step is to build a rough model of the chassis to get a feel for the layout of the axles. Then you can work out how and where to place the drivetrain. But your main priority should be making sure the train can run through curves and switches.

Complex chassis for a steam engine with 2-8-2 wheel arrangement (BR 41 during development)

ATTACHING LEADING AND TRAILING WHEELS

Once you've sorted out your driving wheels, the next step is attaching the leading and trailing axles to the chassis. These axles need a lot of space to turn left and right to get through turns and switches.

The leading wheels of a steam engine are typically located close to the steam cylinders. If you use moving piston rods, the steam cylinders must be fixed and cannot pivot. And because the leading axle needs to turn, it's critical to keep a lot of space between the steam cylinders. Test your chassis on a curved track to make sure everything runs smoothly.

The challenge for the trailing wheel is making sure it can withstand the push power from the motors in the tender. The trailing wheel must have a stable but flexible attachment.

A fixed leading wheel can be used on a shorter chassis where only one axle of the drive wheels uses regular wheels and the other axles use blind drivers.

Steam cylinders interfere with the leading wheels.

Chassis with fixed leading wheels and blind drivers

USING SPOKED WHEELS FOR STEAM TRAINS

Necessity is the mother of invention—or at least that was the motto in the early 2000s when some train builders needed larger wheels for their steam trains. Starting with the large spoked wheels from some 1970s vintage car sets, some builders simply lathed off the outer flange, and others with better tools created aluminum treads and flanges to fit around the wheels. Those custom flanges and wheels have never been sold officially, but you can find some through LEGO forums.

Vintage LEGO spoked wheel with homemade flange

STEAM ENGINE TRAIN WHEELS FROM THIRD-PARTY VENDORS

If you're looking for more options for steam engine wheels, you might want to try third-party vendors. For example, LEGO fan Ben Fleskes from Portland, Oregon, produces a range of molded plastic train wheels under the name Big Ben Bricks (*www.bigbenbricks.com*). His wheels perfectly match the range of LEGO train wheels. The following four sizes are available:

- **Small:** Diameter 0.7 inches (17.6 mm), the same size as the small wheel from the Gray Era.
- **Medium:** Diameter 0.94 inches (24.0 mm), the same size as the larger wheel from the Gray Era.
- **Large:** Diameter 1.2 inches (30.4 mm), available with or without flange, the same size as the large Power Functions wheel.
- **Extra Large:** Diameter 1.45 inches (36.8 mm), counter weight. Has no equivalent in the official LEGO range.

Every Big Ben (BB) wheel has a Technic cross-hole in the middle, and apart from the smallest, they all have an offset pin hole for connecting rods and piston rods. BB wheels do not have a groove for fitting a rubber band, so they risk wheelspin with heavy loads.

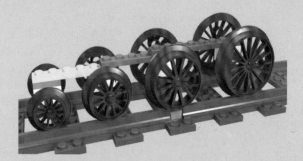

Train wheels produced by Big Ben Bricks

The German class 23 steam engine has a 2-6-2 wheel arrangement. This means it has three driving axles with a leading and a trailing axle. For my model, I've used BB wheels in sizes S, XL, and M.

**Big Ben Bricks train wheels in sizes S, XL, and M
used on my BR 23 model**

Shupp's Brick Train Stuff (*www.shapeways.com/shops/shupp-s-brick-train-stuff*) also offers a variety of LEGO-compatible 3D-printed wheels, including XXL train wheels that are even larger than the XL wheels from Big Ben Bricks.

**Comparing Big Ben Bricks'
XL wheel (red) with Shupp's
XXL wheel (black)**

A FLEXIBLE DESIGN

Another challenge involves the body panels that cover part of the leading or trailing wheels in the prototype—for example, streamlined steam engines like the BR 10 or BR 18. How can you build those in a LEGO model? The leading and trailing wheels can't touch the body panels when they move sideways in curves. The only answer is to attach the panels to the articulated parts so they move with the wheels. You then have to make sure that they don't jam and derail the train.

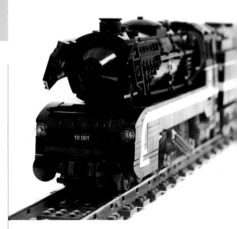

**Partially covered leading
wheels**

RODS AND CYLINDERS

In real-life steam trains, the piston rods transfer the power from the steam cylinders to the driving wheels and convert the reciprocating motion of the pistons into a rotating motion of the wheels. The wheels themselves are linked by the connecting rods to distribute power to all wheels.

In a LEGO model, these rods may not perform their original function, but the mechanical movements are always an eye catcher.

Connecting rods, piston rods, pistons, and steam cylinders on a steam engine

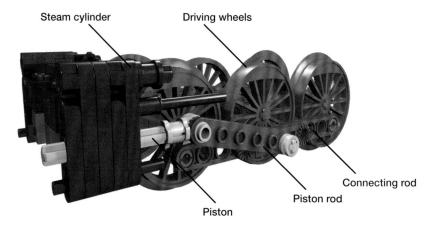

Steam cylinder   Driving wheels

Connecting rod

Piston rod

Piston

Driving wheels with 90° offset

When using connecting rods, you'll need to attach them to pin holes in the wheels. All steam engine train wheels from both LEGO and Big Ben Bricks, apart from the smallest size, have a pin hole exactly one stud away from the center cross-hole. That means the connecting rods move a total of two studs back and forth during the rotation of the driving wheel.

The driving wheels on a steam engine must be *quartered*, meaning the connecting points for the connecting rods are at a 90° (quarter-turn) offset. This ensures smooth motion and prevents the connecting rods from jamming.

LEGO piston rods existed in the Blue Era, and there was a connecting rod for the Gray Era 12 V motor, but those parts are too short for the large wheels. Building your own means using Technic parts, but the width of these assemblies is a problem. Putting connecting rods on the wheels takes the width from 6 studs to 8 studs, and adding the piston rods makes that 10 studs—meaning the steam cylinder assembly also needs to be 10 studs wide.

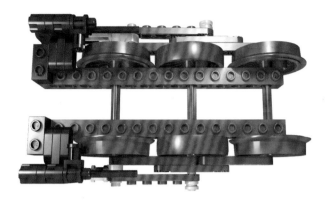

Connecting and piston rods make a steam engine very wide.

These widths are based on using Technic beams and connectors, all of which are one stud wide. If the undercarriage is this wide, the body also needs to be wide for the overall proportions to look good. That means the driver's cab ends up being eight or nine studs wide with a 5- or 6-stud-wide boiler. A model that wide offers a lot of possibilities for adding details.

Connecting and piston rods on the BR 10 steam engine

If the engine has to be narrower than 10 studs, you'll have to trim down the width of the rods. There are some parts that can help with that:

- Rods can be made from thin Technic liftarms or plates with holes at the ends, which are half the width of the beams.
- The Technic Flex system is another popular solution for making narrow rods. The Flex system was used in only a few Technic sets in the 1990s, and they are rare and expensive.

Useful parts for making connecting and piston rods

POWER AND CONTROL

The power system you decide to use for a particular design might depend on the characteristics of the model and the track system.

To build a functional model, look at the drivetrain first. The body shell can be built around the power components later. Consider the following questions:

- Will the power source be onboard, or will you use a powered track?
- Will you use the standard train motor or a self-built drivetrain?
- How long and heavy will the train be?
- How many motors will be needed?

TRAIN MOTORS AND POWERED RAILS

The 12 V motors from the Blue and Gray Eras and the motor from the 9 Volt Era get their power from metal rails. These motors can be placed under a train as one of the trucks. Smaller locomotives can be built right on top of the motor, which is ideal for designing a train because no other power components have to be included.

When you need more motors, you can add them to the train without concern for the train's running direction. The polarity of the track determines the motor's direction.

POWER FUNCTIONS TRAIN MOTORS

When you use Power Functions motors, you have to house the battery box and receiver in the model. When space is tight in the engine, you can house components in a tender (coal car) or on the first car behind the engine.

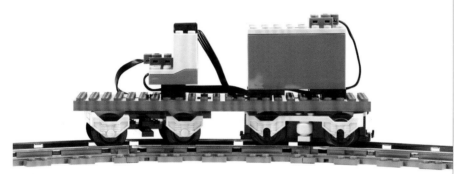

Basic Power Functions setup

You can even move all drive components to a car that pushes the locomotive.

When your locomotive needs two Power Functions train motors on a single channel, you must connect one motor through a polarity switch (#8869) so it runs in the other direction.

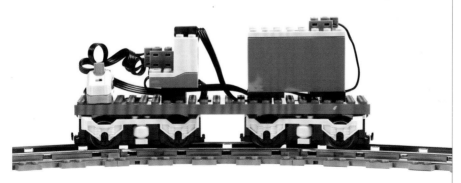

Power Functions setup with two train motors

In a two-motor setup, the train motors must be mounted in opposite directions under the train so that each motor's cable is oriented toward the center of the train's baseplate, where the holes for the cables are located. Because of this orientation, "forward" would have both motors trying to move in opposite directions. The polarity switch fixes this problem. (Unfortunately, the train motor itself doesn't have a direction-changing switch. But if you're willing to make modifications, you can open the train motor housing and use a soldering iron to reverse the wires on the electric motor.)

Motors must be oriented in opposite directions for cables to reach through the holes in the baseplate.

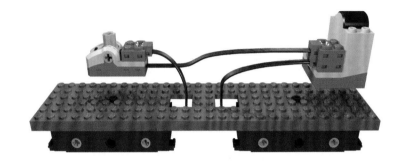

POWER FUNCTIONS DRIVETRAIN

Not all Power Functions motors are designed for trains, but all of them can be used for trains. To use a motor designed for another purpose, transfer the power from the motor to the wheels using Technic elements like axles and gears. The gears perform two functions: routing the drivetrain through the model and increasing or decreasing the speed.

A Power Functions drivetrain using the M motor

When choosing your motor, think about which train motors can give you the most speed.

LEGO Technic elements weren't designed for prolonged use under high loads. They suffer under the force of the bigger Power Functions motors and when trains run for long periods of time. When building drivetrains with LEGO Technic:

- Keep the number of gears as low as possible. With every pair of gears, some of the motor power is lost.
- Secure the axles so the gears can't slip.
- Use short axles. The torque of the motors can warp longer axles, resulting in more loss of power.
- Make sure all axles can spin freely. Take care when putting the geartrain together and keep testing during the build.

You can use any train wheel with a Technic cross-hole to drive the train. When you use bigger wheels, powering only one axle is often enough; the other axles will be connected with connecting rods or will just move from contact with the rails.

Building a drivetrain for small train wheels isn't easy. When using small train wheels, consider using the train motor. When Technic-savvy builders need a powered truck with three axles, they create a custom drivetrain. If you attempt to make your own drivetrain, you'll have to overcome the following:

- Only small gears can be used on the wheel axles.
- Three-axle trucks need one axle to slide sideways and navigate tight curves.
- The axle that transfers the power from the motor to the wheels is also the pivot for the truck itself, so the force of the motor could rotate the truck and cause a derailment.

THE SBRICK RECEIVER

SBrick (Smart Brick, *www.sbrick.com*) is an alternative for the Power Functions infrared receiver (#8884). Instead of controlling your trains via infrared using the Power Functions remote control (#8879), the SBrick receiver lets you control your trains via Bluetooth using a smartphone or tablet.

Because it works over Bluetooth instead of infrared, the SBrick can be completely hidden in the model, as it's not necessary to have a line of sight between the controller and receiver.

Power Functions setup using the SBrick receiver

MODELING DETAILS

Details are important when you're creating a realistic-looking train model. In addition to scale, you must consider color, silhouette, windows, pantographs, and other details unique to the real-world train your model is based on.

COLOR

Vintage trains often use darker colors. Those colors exist in the LEGO range, but the selection of available parts is rather limited compared to core colors like red, yellow, blue, black, white, and gray. Take, for example, dark green, a perfect color for many classic trains. According to BrickLink, there are around 600 different parts available in dark green, compared to thousands for yellow and red. A few important parts like the headlight brick are not yet available in dark green, adding to the challenge of creating a LEGO model in this color.

Vintage car in dark green

STREAMLINED FRONT

When designing your own model of a modern railcar or locomotive, the front will likely pose the biggest challenge. Finding just the right slopes and curves to mimic a streamlined shape usually requires some trial and error.

Older locomotives and American freight diesels are much easier to capture. Aerodynamics were not important for those trains, so their design is boxy. These trains also have lots of interesting details like lights, railings, and grilles that can be represented very well in LEGO.

DRIVER'S CABIN

The driver's cabin is the face of a locomotive, so I pay a lot of attention to it when I build a model.

I usually start with the windshield and side windows of the cabin. I look for existing window or windshield parts I can use, and if none fit the bill, I use transparent 1×2 plates. Window frames are thin, so building them in LEGO requires compromises. Luckily there are elements, such as the upright part of various brackets or the square flag, that are half as thin as a plate, a good size for window frames. They add a lot of support elements inside, though, so there won't be any room left for the driver. For an example, see "The Cab" on page 118.

Once the windshield and side windows are in place, adding other details like lights, handrails, and windshield wipers completes the model's appearance.

WINDOWS AND DOORS

LEGO has a few standard train windows and doors (see "Windows and Doors" on page 25), but you can also use windows from other sets.

Modern passenger cars tend to have a band of windows rather than individual ones, and you can create such a band with transparent panels mounted sideways.

When it comes to doors, you must consider whether you want them to be functional. Should you be able to manually open them to enhance play value?

Streamlined front of a bi-level car

Window and window frame of the Vectron's cabin

Should they be operated by remote control? Or is it sufficient to just imply where the doors are?

ROOFS

The roof of a train car, old or new, is usually curved. Fortunately, LEGO offers a nice assortment of curved slope elements that can be used to capture a variety of curved roof profiles.

To enhance the play value, the roof is often built so it can be easily removed for access to the interior of the train. You can use techniques from the Modular Buildings series (a combination of studs and tiles) to achieve this.

Removable roof of a bi-level car

CORRIDOR CONNECTORS

Another typical element of a passenger car is the corridor connector, which allows passengers to walk from one car to the next. In real life, these connectors are flexible, so they remain closed even when the train goes through curves.

In LEGO, it is impossible to model this flexibility; the function can only be implied. The connectors should be built so that they're as close together as possible on straight sections of track without touching each other through curves and switches.

PANTOGRAPHS

Pantographs are roof-mounted structures on an electric locomotive or railcar that transfer electrical power from overhead cables. In Gray Era sets, pantographs were made of plates and looked rather primitive. A special pantograph part was introduced in the 1990s, but it looks best on 6-wide trains.

Pantograph made from minifigure accessories

With a little creativity, you can make a pantograph from various LEGO parts. Minifigure accessories like pistols, ice skates, or even minifig hands are often used to build pantographs. The pirate captain's hook also works well with Flex-tubes and bars.

UNDERFRAMES

The area below the floor of a locomotive or wagon, or *underframe*, can't be ignored. A train with only trucks below the floor will look rather bare. Depending on the era and the type of train, you'll find all sorts of details under the train, such as truss rods and auxiliary equipment like battery boxes, tanks, pressure cylinders, pipes, and hoses.

Modern trains like to hide all that behind streamlined panels, so just like on the roofs of these models, various curved pieces can be used here instead.

A realistic underframe on a passenger car

TRACK DESIGN AND LAYOUT

Traveling in comfort on a train means passengers shouldn't feel the centrifugal forces when the train goes through curves. To achieve that, the train should travel in straight lines as much as possible. Where curves are necessary, they have a very large radius—for example, full-speed curves for the German ICE high-speed train have a 2.5 mile radius. Even for slow-speed switching, the minimum curve radius for a modern locomotive is around 300 feet.

For a serious railway modeler, those radii are impractical, and they're nearly impossible in LEGO. That 300-foot radius in L-gauge scale (1:38) would be 296 studs (7.8 feet; 240 centimeters). Compare that to standard LEGO curved track, which has a radius of 40 studs (1 foot; 32 centimeters).

TIPS FOR CURVES

Without resorting to cutting, it's just not that easy to change the geometry of the standard LEGO track elements. There are two options for gentler curves that are becoming more popular: a Grand Curve, which cleverly curves straight track, and track from third-party manufacturers like ME Models and BrickTracks.

The jumper forces the straight line into a curve.

GRAND CURVE

Despite the strong, stable connection between track pieces, there's still a bit of play, so it's actually not that easy to make a long stretch of track perfectly straight. This led to the idea that straight pieces could be "bent" gradually into what's known as a Grand Curve.

Using 1×2 jumper plates that give a half-stud offset, you can force straight pieces into a curve, or rather a really big polygon. On the inside, the track pieces are connected with a normal plate, while on the outside the jumper forces a half-stud gap, big enough to create an angle but not big enough to interrupt the electrical connection of 9 V track.

LEGO trains require lots of space. This large-radius curve uses straight track pieces.

The Grand Curve method requires a lot of space. The radius of the polygon is 238 studs (6.2 feet; 190 centimeters), six times bigger than the standard curve. They also take more parts—92 straight track pieces for a full circle compared to the 16 curved pieces for a standard circle. Having seen my train go through these curves, though, I have to say it's worth the effort.

RAILS FROM ME MODELS

ME Models (*www.me-models.com*), started by Mike Fetsko and Eric Olson, produces curved track, consisting of separate rails and crossties, in four radii:

- **R56:** Radius 56 studs (1.5 feet; 45 centimeters)
- **R72:** Radius 72 studs (1.9 feet; 58 centimeters)
- **R88:** Radius 88 studs (2.3 feet; 70 centimeters)
- **R104:** Radius 104 studs (2.7 feet; 83 centimeters)

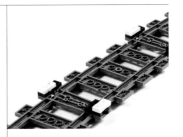

Track connections seen from below

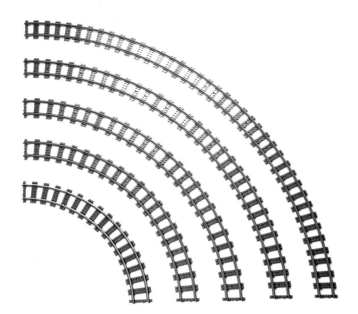

Curved track from ME Models in different radii, with standard LEGO track for comparison (the innermost track)

The radii have been chosen so that the distance between the crossties of two curves is always eight studs. They are available in dark bluish gray, black, dark brown, and reddish brown. As well as the curved rails, ME Models offers straight rails in 8-, 16-, and 32-stud lengths.

ME Models produces these parts in both plastic and metal. The metal rails have a fishplate connection similar to normal model railway track, which is not compatible with LEGO track, so you'll need a conversion piece (available in 8-stud length) to connect ME Models track to LEGO track.

The ME Models track is similar to Blue Era track, both in the profile of the rails (an inverted T shape) and in the fact that individual rails are placed on 2×8 crosstie plates. Unfortunately, the production tolerances are not on the same level as LEGO, so the connection between rails and crossties is not always stable, and it takes some patience to put the track together. Once the track is built and placed on a flat surface, the trains run very well. But even ME Models recommends gluing the rails to the crossties to stabilize sections of track.

RAILS FROM OTHER THIRD-PARTY MANUFACTURERS

Scott Hoffmeyer at BrickTracks (*www.shapeways.com/shops/ltracks*) uses 3D printing to make custom-shaped track elements, such as large crossover switches with a radius of 104 studs. 4D Brix (*www.4dbrix.com*) is another third-party manufacturer, offering narrow-gauge and monorail track segments in addition to curves, straight segments, and switches.

BALLASTING TRACK

There is more to making your LEGO train layout look like a model railway than just realistic-looking trains. You can also improve upon the track itself.

Black or brown 1×1 and 1×4 tiles are often used to model wooden crossties. To get them at a 1-stud interval, you first need to fill in the gaps between the 2×8 crossties produced by LEGO. This conversion is not difficult, but it's very parts-intensive. The result, however, is a much better-looking track with more contrast than the standard gray/gray combination.

When you start to think about bridges, you have to consider inclines. As in real life, LEGO trains do not like steep inclines. For light trains, going up by one plate per track segment is fine, but my heavier 8-wide models prefer an even gentler incline of 1 plate per 1.5 track segments.

For the track bed, you could use a layer of basic bricks that are sloped down into the surrounding landscape with roof bricks or stepped layers of plates. For landscaping around the track, the only limit is your imagination.

ME Models track with ballast and crossties based on instructions from *www.l-gauge.org*

If all that sounds like too much work, you could simply start by putting 1×1 plates in black, gray, and dark tan on the crossties to model ballast gravel.

PLAN YOUR LAYOUT WITH BLUEBRICK

The free open source software BlueBrick (*bluebrick.lswproject.com*), written by Alban Nanty, is a tool for planning track layouts with baseplates, streets, and tables. It includes LEGO track elements from all eras as well as ME Models track. It is very easy to use, and you can even add your own custom parts.

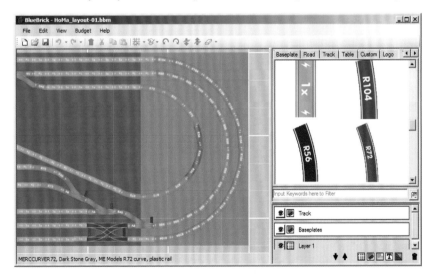

Planning a track layout with BlueBrick software

In the next chapter, I'll cover more design techniques by walking through the development of a few of my own train models.

CASE STUDIES IN DESIGN

Armed with the tools and knowledge about LEGO modeling covered in the previous chapters, we'll now take a closer look at the actual design process using some of my own builds as a guide.

DESIGNING A MODEL OF A REAL-LIFE TRAIN

Designing a model is a creative and personal process: there's no right or wrong way to build a successful model. The guidelines in this section are meant to get you started. You'll certainly develop your own strategies along the way.

GATHERING INFORMATION ABOUT THE ORIGINAL

A good way to start a new design is to gather information about the original (or *prototype*) train. It's easier now than ever to find information about any train online—no matter how rare it is, a Google image search will return some relevant pictures. Ideally, you should get photos from all angles. If you want exact proportions, it can't hurt to track down blueprints, which are surprisingly easy to find.

Vectron electric locomotive by Siemens

Naapříč Evropou
Európán keresztül
Quer durch Europa
de-a lungul Europei
Europą wzdłuż i wszerz
Naprieč Európou

■□ Cargo

An important design element is the *livery*, or the distinctive color scheme and logos used by the railway company or companies who used the prototype. Consider the different liveries used by different railway companies or in different periods, and which LEGO colors are the best match for those liveries.

Then you'll want to dig into the details. What's the wheel layout? What sort of drivetrain does the real engine have? How are the roof, windows, corridor connectors, and other elements designed and built? Which of those elements are essential? And which ones can be left out?

SET YOURSELF A CHALLENGE

Having some constraints can guide your creativity. I find it helpful to set some targets for a new model right at the start. For example:

- Decide on a scale and choose the width: 6-, 7-, or 8-wide?
- Decide how the train will be powered and what type of track it'll run on.
- Choose a target audience: should it be a realistic, recognizable model, or are play functions more important?

FIRST DRAFT

You don't sit down and build a new model from scratch in one go. That's where creating your own model is very different from building an official LEGO set.

Typically, you start building your first design, and then you improve it over a number of iterations. Sometimes, though, a project is left on the shelf for a while, waiting for a new flash of inspiration to finish it.

There are different approaches you can take to designing your model:

- Play with bricks (work with just a single color or explore various color schemes).
- Sketch with pencil and paper.
- Create digital designs using software like LEGO Digital Designer, MLCad, or LDCad.
- Break the model down into components to see which ones are easy and which ones are going to be difficult.

Experience will tell you which approaches work best for you. Whatever medium you choose, keep your various drafts. Start every sketch on a new sheet of paper or a new file, and build the iterations side by side rather than dismantling or changing the previous versions. Sometimes the best ideas come right at the start and you'll want to revisit them.

Personally, I prefer to start with physical bricks right away, with pictures of the prototype in front of me. By actually building, I can get a feel for the stability of the connections, which is hard to get from a digital model.

I often consider which part of the train will be the most complex or difficult and start there. For modern trains, the streamlined front is usually the hardest, while for historical steam engines, it tends to be the undercarriage with its various wheels and rods. It can take a few long nights of experimenting to create a chassis that runs properly through switches and curves. Only when I'm happy with these first components do I progress to the rest of the model.

Always start with the hardest part.

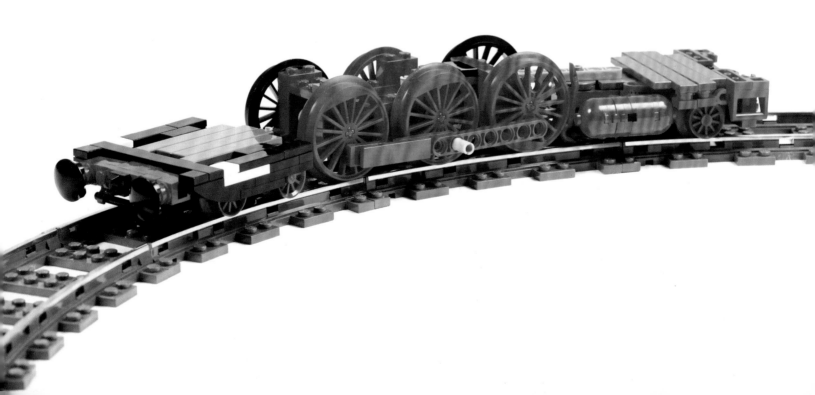

SECOND DRAFT

In the second phase, the most difficult questions have already been answered, so now you can work on refining the model. If you have focused only on individual components so far, this is the time to combine them to see if they all work together.

If you haven't tested the model on track yet, now is the time to do so. If you're building a complete train, you'll need to test the whole train, not just individual locomotives and wagons, to make sure the combination can move through switches. You may need to change the pivot points of trucks and couplings.

Time for details

FINAL MODEL

The number of iterations your design process takes is entirely up to you. Maybe the second draft is already good enough that you can start ordering parts in the right colors. Or maybe you find that it has problems when it runs—for example, it's not unusual for a completed model to have difficulty getting through switches, even though the bare chassis ran well when you tested it on its own.

Know when to stop. You'll reach a point where the model looks good and runs well, and any further changes won't make it a better model.

When the structure is complete, it's time to add the finishing touches, such as stickers. Stickers, when applied in the right amount, can make a model look more realistic, whether you get them from a LEGO set or design and print your own. You can print your designs on blank sticker sheets or on paper that you apply with rubber cement or similar glues. I've found that stickers work better as decoration than they do taking the place of structural components like headlights or door handles.

In the rest of the chapter, I'll share case studies of some of my own model designs so you can see how this approach works in practice.

A well-placed sticker is the finishing touch for a model— as long as it stays in place!

THE REGIONAL-EXPRESS: BOMBARDIER DOUBLE-DECK COACHES

The plan to build a model of a typical German Regional-Express with bi-level passenger cars had been in the back of my mind for a long time. These trains were part of my daily commute, so I know them inside and out.

German Railways Regional-Express using Bombardier double-deck coaches

My model of the Bombardier double-deck coach passenger cars

The bi-level cars built by Bombardier make full use of the available loading gauge to offer a lot of interior space to passengers. The windows at the upper level have a characteristic bend at one-third of their height, following the narrow shape of the upper level. The last car is a control car, meaning it has a full driver cab to control the locomotive at the other end of the train when it is pushing.

THE CHALLENGES

For this model, I set myself the following challenges:

- Create upper windows with the iconic bend and a red window frame on all sides.
- Build at least three cars, including one with the streamlined driver's cab.
- Scale to 7-wide so the cars do not get too long and heavy and slow down the train.

FIRST DRAFT

For the upper windows, I used the microstriping technique (see "Microstriping" on page 64), as I found no standard LEGO element would do. For the windows at the lower level, I used the classic 4-stud-wide LEGO train windows, and for the doors I used the 2-stud-wide train windows.

I experimented with various window layouts to get the right overall length of the cars. I had to make some compromises around the trucks to prevent the cars from getting too long. The doors are not placed exactly over the trucks, and the trucks themselves are quite short, with only two studs between the wheel holders.

Creating the smooth lines of the cab was a labor of love—the design for the cab took twice as long as the design for all the other parts of the cars combined.

The window layout defines the overall length of the cars.

The streamlined driver cab of the control car

FINISHING TOUCHES

After overcoming the challenge of the driver cab, I continued with some easier elements: a ceiling over the vestibule, and stairs to allow the minifigs to go to their seats on the upper or lower level.

The original train features a destination sign between the two rows of windows. To give the side of the cars a bit of texture, I decided to recess the signs by half a stud. They are built with sideways tiles that are half a plate lower than a brick, so the thin end of a bracket is used to fill the gap.

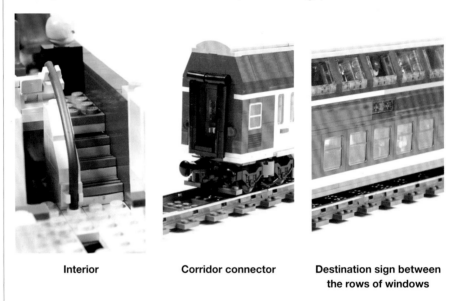

| Interior | Corridor connector | Destination sign between the rows of windows |

The test drive had to wait another few weeks, as I first had to build the locomotive.

SIEMENS VECTRON ELECTRIC LOCOMOTIVE

The Regional-Express cars needed a suitable engine to complete the train. I decided on the Siemens Vectron electric locomotive because of its unusual grille below the windshield, which supplies fresh air to the air-conditioning units. In real life, this engine is mostly used for freight trains, but I thought it would look good with my Regional-Express. DB Schenker in Poland has a few Vectrons in the typical bright red livery.

Siemens Vectron electric locomotive used by DB Schenker Rail Polska

My model of the Siemens Vectron electric locomotive

THE CHALLENGES

I set myself these challenges for this model:

- Model the angled grilles in the front.
- Scale to 7-wide to allow for detail.
- Include two Power Functions train motors with receiver and rechargeable battery, all onboard.

THE CAB

After studying many images of the original and building a few sketches, I realized it would be impossible to model all the angles of the cab. I decided to focus on re-creating the characteristic angled grilles, and I didn't want to use a prebuilt LEGO piece to do that. Here's a look at the end result.

Details of the cab

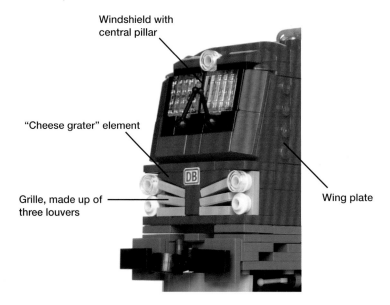

Windshield with central pillar

"Cheese grater" element

Grille, made up of three louvers

Wing plate

Here's how I put it together. The first element I decided to use was the cheese grater ("Slope 18 2×1×2/3 with Four Slots"), which I mounted upside down in order to define the angled top of the grilles. Because the slopes are mounted upside down, a lot of other parts in the front are, as well.

"Cheese grater" elements
brace the gray grille on top.

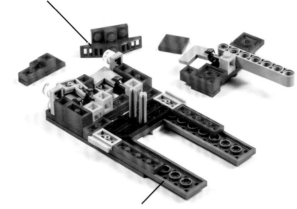

Sometimes you'll find you need to
build upside down.

Cab, interior view. The
second louver of the grille
is a corner tile!

"Bar 1L with Clip Mechanical Claw" holds
the second and third louvers at an angle.

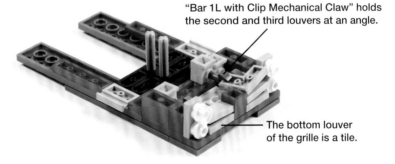

The bottom louver
of the grille is a tile.

The front of the cab and grille
in process

A black flag forms a microstripe
for the center pillar.

Hinge bricks mount the black flag
and the angled windshield section.

The components that make up
the upper part of the cab

119

For the windshield, I decided to use transparent 1×2 plates, the most flexible method for creating windows, and oriented them sideways. I filled the 5-stud width of the windshield area with 10 vertical transparent plates and a black tile on either side. That left a half-plate gap in the middle, which I filled with the edge of a black 2×2 flag to create the center pillar of the windshield. This setup looked neat from the outside but chaotic on the inside.

The front is slowly taking shape.

Black flag edge used
as a center pillar

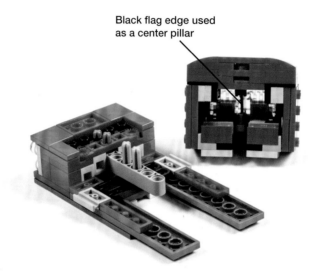

This windshield assembly had to be mounted at an angle, which I accomplished using 1×2 hinge bricks. The side uses 2×4 wing plates—luckily the original does not have side windows in that location.

DOORS WITH SIDE HANDRAILS

Next, I built the doors. The doors are two studs wide with a thin black frame created with brackets. The handrails are constructed from alternating standard 1×2 plates and 1×2 plates with handles.

The door, from the outside

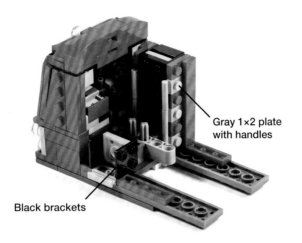

Gray 1×2 plate
with handles

Black brackets

Black brackets are used for
the thin black frame of the
side doors.

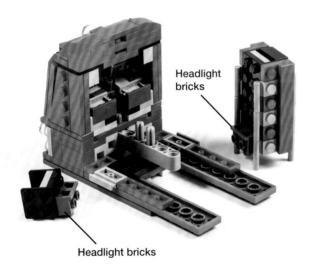

Headlight
bricks

Headlight bricks

The doors are attached to the
upside-down baseplate with
headlight bricks.

THE TRUCKS

The trucks posed the usual challenge of building in 7-wide: building the details around the 4-stud-wide train motor body. With limited space, the only option was to use the pin on the motor as the pivot for the trucks. Buffers and couplings had to be attached to the trucks so the locomotive wouldn't lose its cars when traveling along tight curves.

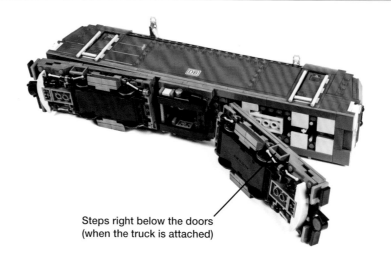

Steps right below the doors
(when the truck is attached)

With the motors placed quite far back from the front of the engine, there
was enough room between the motor and the buffer to add some details, like
the steps below the cab doors.

FULL POWER

The rechargeable battery (#8878), the receiver (#8884), the polarity switch
(#8869), and lots of Power Functions cable easily filled the available space in
the middle of the car, much like the engine in the original.

Electric locomotives need pantographs on the roof to get their power, and the Vectron comes with either two or four. Because of the limited space that was available, I opted for the version with two.

The pantographs were made with a collection of repurposed parts:

- Ice skates from the old Belville theme
- Minifig pistols as bars
- Short pieces of pneumatic tube that fit over the barrels of the guns

FINAL THOUGHTS

The finished model is now 40 studs long without buffers and couplings and looks a bit stocky compared to the original. At 7-wide, the correct to-scale length would be 44 studs, so in the future I might rework the model to add two or four studs to see what effect that would have.

STEAM ENGINE BR 10

Back in 2001, before dedicated steam engine wheels were available, I built a model of a BR 10 steam engine (BR stands for *Baureihe*, meaning "class" or "series"). I used old spoked wheels with custom-made aluminum flanges (see "Using Spoked Wheels for Steam Trains" on page 89). The piston rods on the model were not functional, and connecting rods were not possible at all.

However, the two 9 V train motors under the tender give the locomotive a lot of power, and my "Riviera Express" is still running today.

When steam engine wheels became available, I decided to revisit this design and update it to include the new wheels, as well as working connecting and piston rods.

My BR 10 models from 2001 (left) and 2016 (right) head to head

My model of a German BR 10 steam engine

BR 10 001 at the German Steam Engine Museum in Neuenmarkt

THE ORIGINAL

The BR 10 was the last steam engine developed in Germany. Diesel and electric were already being used as efficient alternatives to steam in 1957, when only two of these locomotives were built by Krupp in Essen.

The BR 10 has a 4-6-2 wheel configuration, meaning it has two leading axles, three axles with large driving wheels and a single trailing axle, and then a tender with two trucks. Notable features of this locomotive are the streamlined paneling that partially covers the wheels and the cone-shaped front of the boiler.

THE CHALLENGES

I set myself a number of challenges for this model:

- Update the old model to have working rods.
- Use Big Ben Bricks XL wheels for the drivers.
- Model the streamlined paneling so that the locomotive can still run through curves and switches.
- Use Power Functions with battery, receiver, and two train motors in the tender.

THE UNDERCARRIAGE

When building a LEGO steam engine, it's best to start with the chassis and wheels. It can be quite a challenge to get it to run reliably without derailments.

The undercarriage of the BR 10

Using a scaled side view, I worked out the position of the axles of the loco-motive and tender. My first attempt, with six studs between the large wheels, did not look right and the locomotive ended up too short. A 7-stud distance, however, is too long, so I ended up in the middle with a distance of 6.5 studs. Using the Technic 1×1 and 1×2 bricks with holes directly below the studs, I was able to achieve that distance, but it meant I had to find a creative solution for the connecting rods.

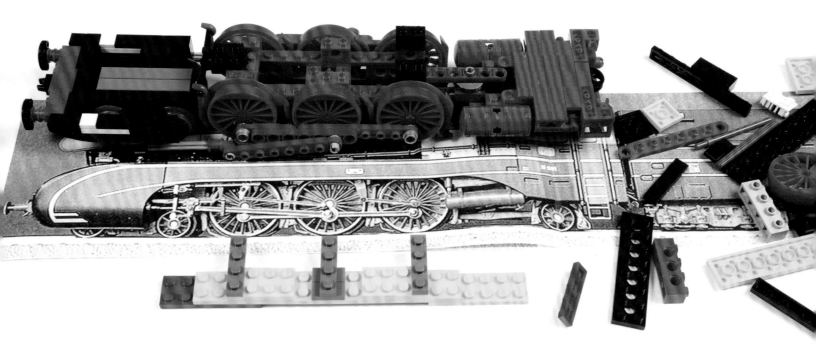

Working out the wheel spacing with a scaled image of the prototype

A LEGO train with three fixed axles won't get through the curves, so the solution is to use a so-called *blind driver*, a train wheel without a flange, that does not touch the rails. On my old BR 10, the third axle could pivot, as it had no connecting rods.

DRIVING WHEELS: FIRST TRY

Having established the axle spacing, I tried building a chassis. The first two axles were fixed to the chassis while the third one could pivot, so I could use flanged wheels on all three axles. There was even enough space between the wheels to model the brakes. On the real train, the brake pads are pushed directly onto the wheels, and I used minifig crowbars to model these brake levers.

Undercarriage of the BR 10, first attempt (seen from below)

The odd spacing between the axles is an almost insurmountable challenge for the connecting rods. Add a pivoting axle to the mix, and it becomes practically impossible to attach connecting rods. After a few attempts, I found a solution that let me attach connecting rods to the first two wheels but not the third.

On my workbench, this construction ran well through the test curve, but the first test on a proper test track was a sobering experience and showed me that this solution just wasn't good enough. It had a tendency to derail on turns because the first large wheel jumped the rails.

DRIVING WHEELS: SECOND TRY

I had to start over from scratch. For the next version, I focused on the leading wheels, thinking their flanges may be too small to prevent derailments. I tried Gray Era train wheels with bigger flanges, but they did not resolve the issue.

Back to the drivers, I tried a solution with three fixed axles. This configuration resulted in a lot of friction in curves, but it did run without derailment. Of course this means using blind drivers on the middle axle, which doesn't look the best but is necessary to make it run.

Undercarriage of the BR 10, second attempt (seen from below)

PISTONS AND RODS

Eventually I found an elegant solution for the connecting rods that accommodates the odd axle spacing. To avoid the extremely hard to find red 1×8 Technic plates, you can use an alternative solution with thin beams and more common 1×4 Technic plates.

Detail showing the connecting and piston rods (alternative build)

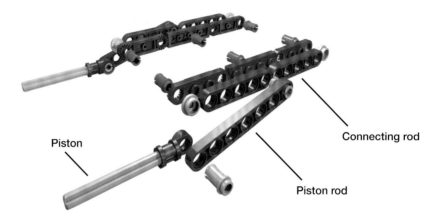

Piston

Connecting rod

Piston rod

Between these fixed axles, crowbars fit nicely for the brake system. And finally, this chassis runs convincingly on the test track. It may not go very fast through the curves and switches, but as long as I am sensible with the speed, it is reliable.

LEADING AND TRAILING AXLES

I found the pivot point for the leading truck and trailing axle once again by trial and error. Thanks to a clever Technic part, "Technic, Pin 3L Center Pin Hole," I could place the pivot points directly on the first and last driving axles.

The piston rods, like the driving wheels, must be connected to the main chassis. The steam cylinders themselves are hidden behind the body panels on the prototype, so they didn't need to be modeled. It was sufficient to use some Technic 1×2 bricks with two holes to hold the pistons and make them "disappear" inside the body panels.

The connection of the trailing axle had to be strong because it has to transfer the pushing power of the motors in the tender to the locomotive.

The two red pressure cylinders right in front of the trailing wheels are held only by a single 1×1 plate with a clip.

The pivot point for the leading and trailing axles is directly below the driving axles.

Exploded view of the pressure cylinders

SHAPING THE BODY

The characteristic body panels on the BR 10 are decorated with silver striping. Guided by the motto "bricks are better than stickers," I decided to create them using white LEGO bricks.

Body panels on the BR 10 covering part of the undercarriage

THE BOILER

For the boiler, I used some curved slopes, which got me closer to the round shape than the inverted slopes and rounded bricks I used previously. A number of bars and hoses add detail.

The boiler of the BR 10

For the smokestack, I combined a car tire and a 2×2 radar dish. I used the tiny "Tile, Round 1×1 with Pin" to connect it solidly to the top of the boiler.

Detail of the smokestack

THE DRIVER'S CAB

The concept of *Einheitsloks*, or "standard locomotives," is most obvious in the driver's cab. While the various German steam engine designs of this era often have unique wheel configurations, they all share a lot of standard components for the cab. For the LEGO model, that also means there are not many alternatives to choose from, so I used some tried-and-true constructions from my BR 23, BR 80, and first BR 10 models.

The thin white stripe below the windows is not a sticker but the white top half of a 1×2 hinge brick.

Driver's cab

THE TENDER

Luckily, I had enough parts left in my collection to continue the thin stripe along the tender. The sides of the trucks and the back of the tender are more detailed than on the first model, but they're still not too exciting. It was easy to find space for the battery box and receiver in the 8-wide body of the tender.

The only tricky bit was working out the pivot point for the connection with the trailing axle of the engine. I wanted to couple the tender as close as possible to the locomotive while also allowing them to run on tight curves and switches without colliding or derailing. The solution was to experiment with different lengths of Technic plates until I settled on a 1x5 Technic plate, which is less error-prone when running this engine.

The tender of the BR 10

BUILDING INSTRUCTIONS FOR THE BR 10
You can download the building instructions for this BR 10 steam engine at *www.nostarch.com/legotrains*.

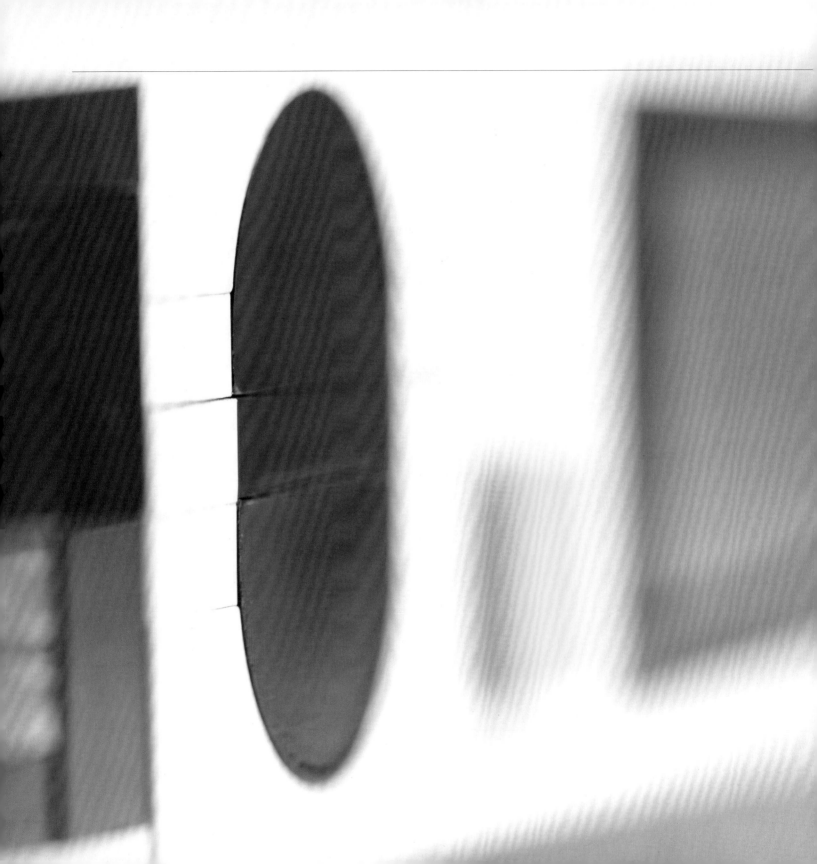

BUILDING INSTRUCTIONS!

Get inspired with these step-by-step instructions for building an Inter-City Express, a simple gondola, a Swiss Electric Locomotive Be 6/8 "Crocodile," a vintage passenger car, and a steam engine.

A Deutsche Bahn ICE 3

If following instructions *exactly* is unappealing to you, take these models further and make improvements. You could add headlights and taillights, or even add interior lighting. You might change the scale: make the cars longer or wider, or add more cars. Don't forget about the interior. How about adding some fancier seats or even a restaurant car? Vandalism is common—can you create LEGO graffiti?

FINDING PARTS

Detailed parts lists for all featured models, with BrickLink part numbers, are available at *www.nostarch.com/legotrains*. If you have difficulty finding certain parts, be creative and make your own substitutions.

INTER-CITY EXPRESS

These detailed building instructions for both the driving car and trailer car will help you build a realistic-looking, functioning model of this well-known high-speed train.

FACT SHEET

Idea and design: James Mathis

(*www.brickshelf.com/cgi-bin/gallery.cgi?m=jamathis*)

Difficulty level: Easy

Style: 6-wide

Drive: Power Functions train motor under one of the two driving cars

LEGO model of the
Deutsche Bahn ICE 3

ICE 3 TRAILER CAR

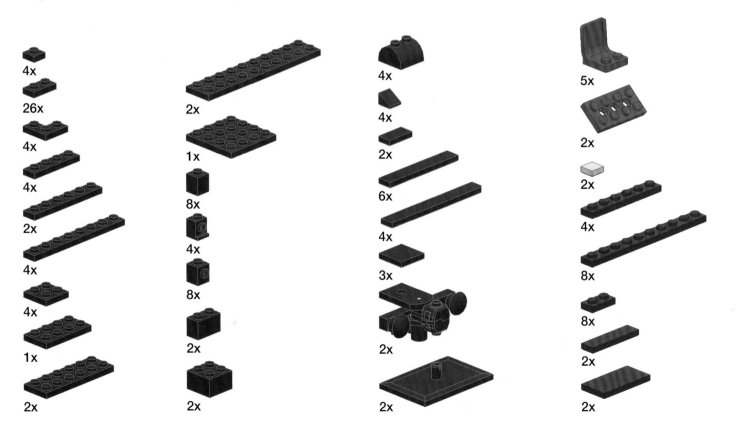

4x

26x

4x

4x

2x

4x

4x

1x

2x

2x

1x

8x

4x

8x

2x

2x

4x

4x

2x

6x

4x

3x

2x

2x

5x

2x

2x

4x

8x

8x

2x

2x

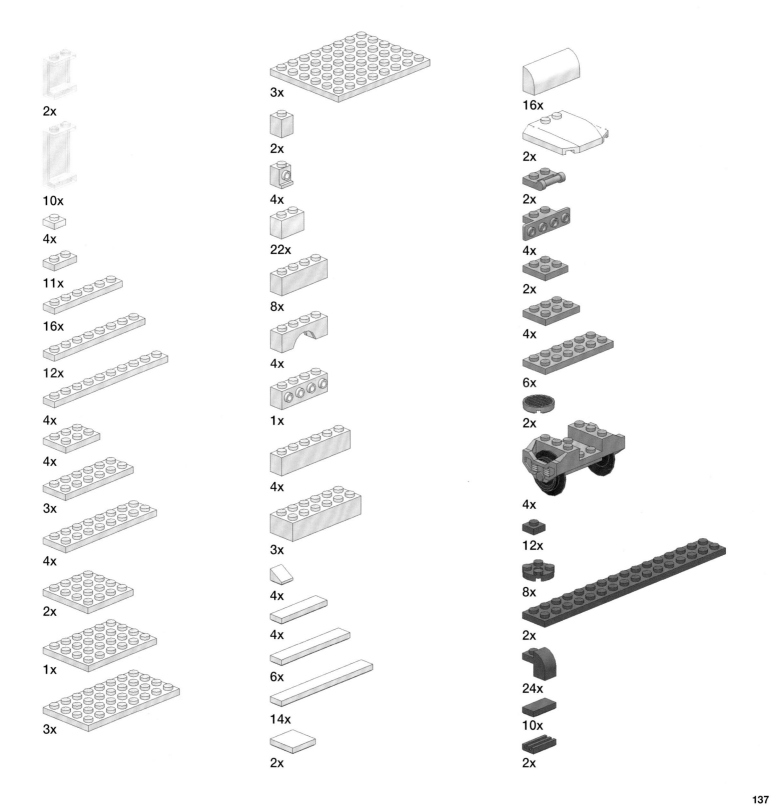

2x

10x

4x

11x

16x

12x

4x

4x

3x

4x

2x

1x

3x

3x

2x

4x

22x

8x

4x

1x

4x

3x

4x

4x

6x

14x

2x

16x

2x

2x

4x

2x

4x

6x

2x

4x

12x

8x

2x

24x

10x

2x

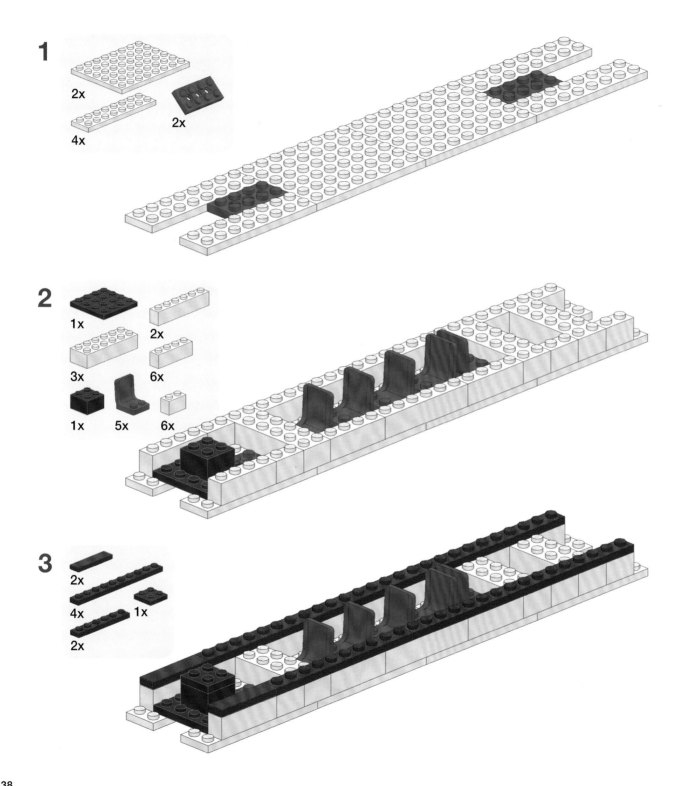

1

2x

4x

2x

2

1x

2x

3x

6x

1x

5x

6x

3

2x

4x 1x

2x

4

4x

2x

1x

5

4x

2x

1x

6

4x

2x

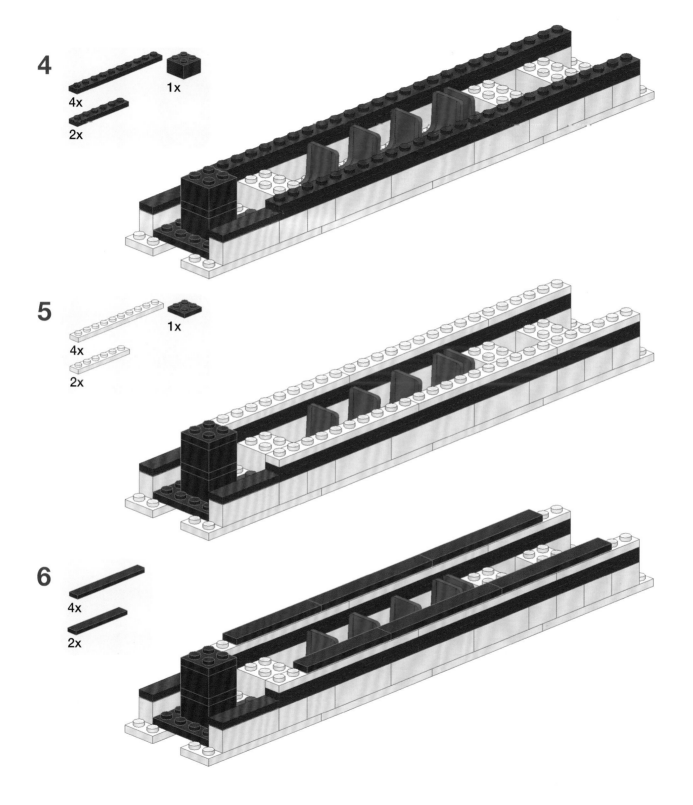

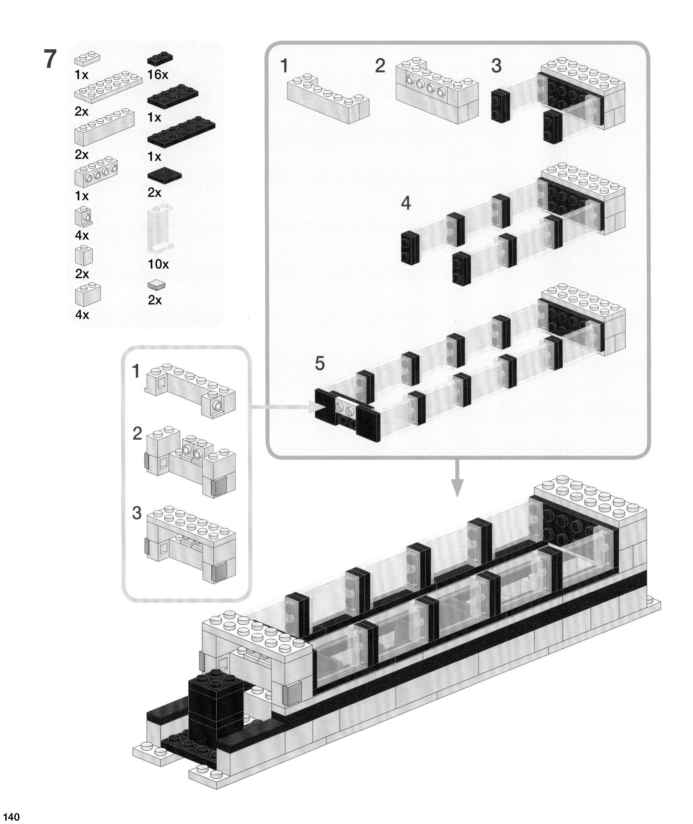

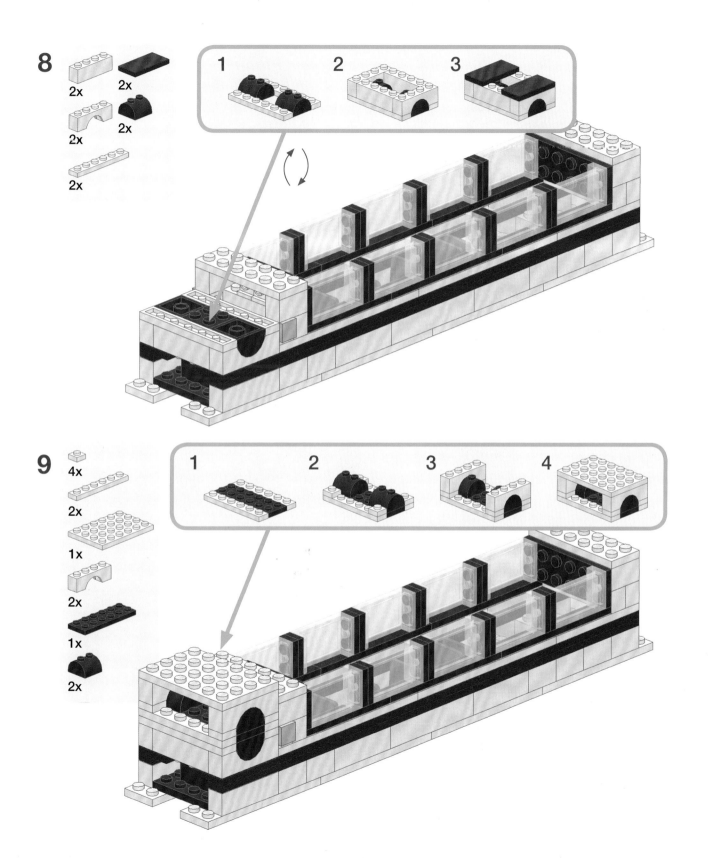

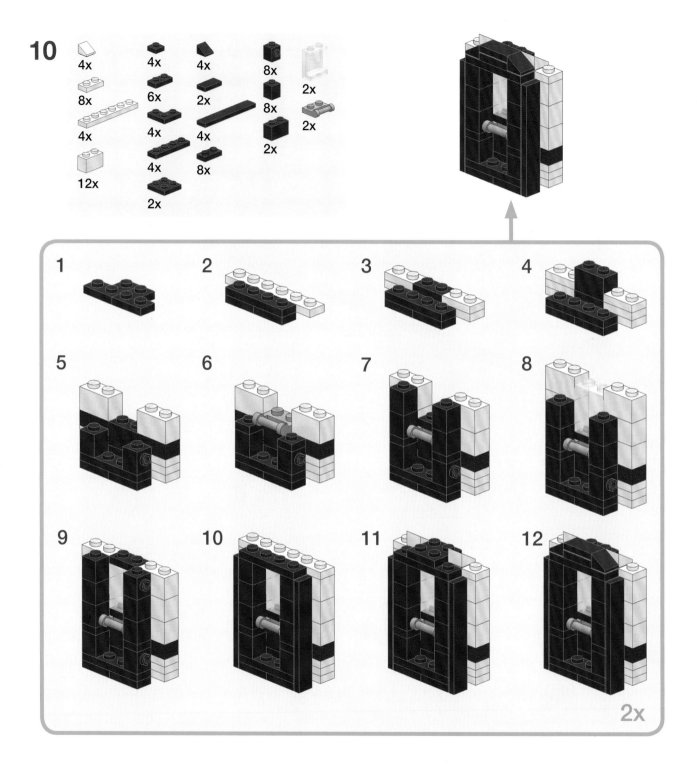

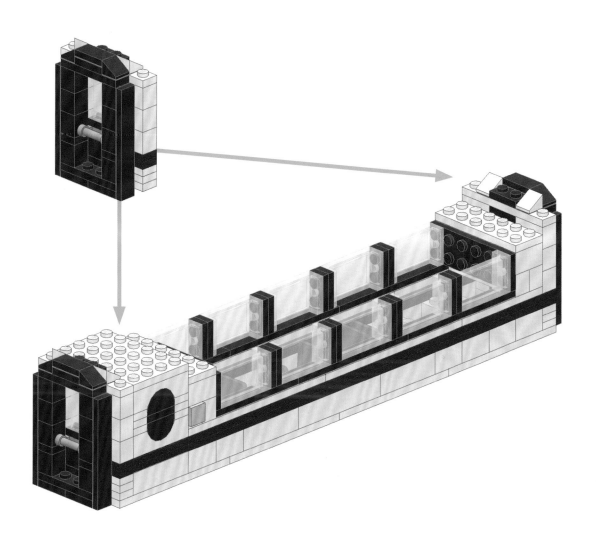

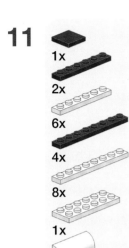

11

1x
2x
6x
4x
8x
1x
16x

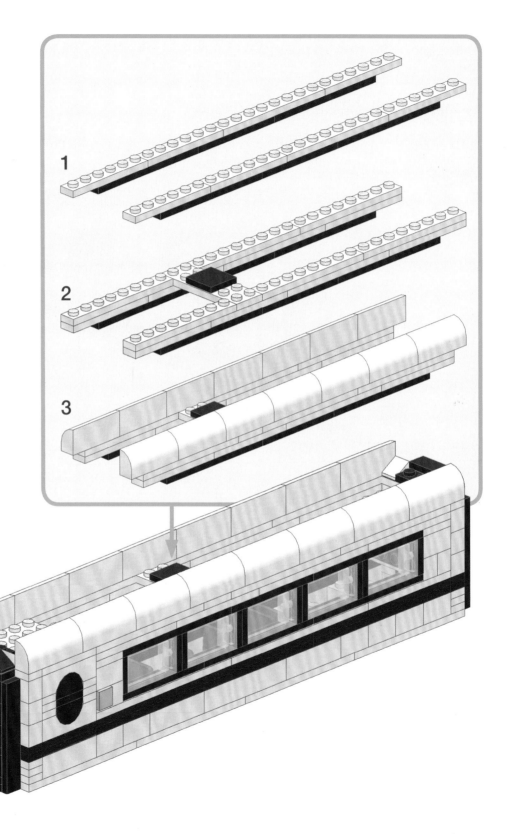

1

2

3

12

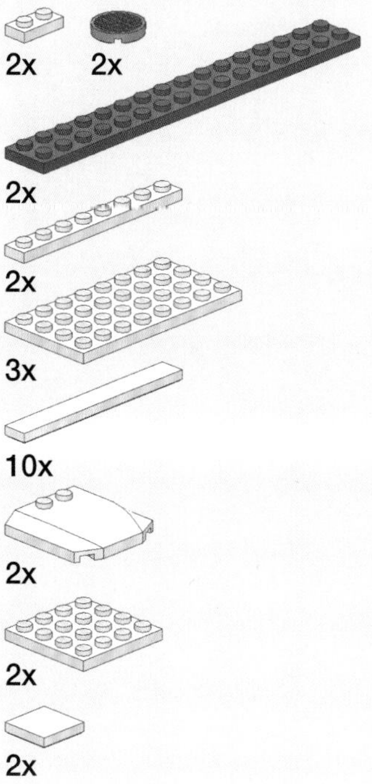

2x 2x

2x

2x

2x

3x

10x

2x

2x

2x

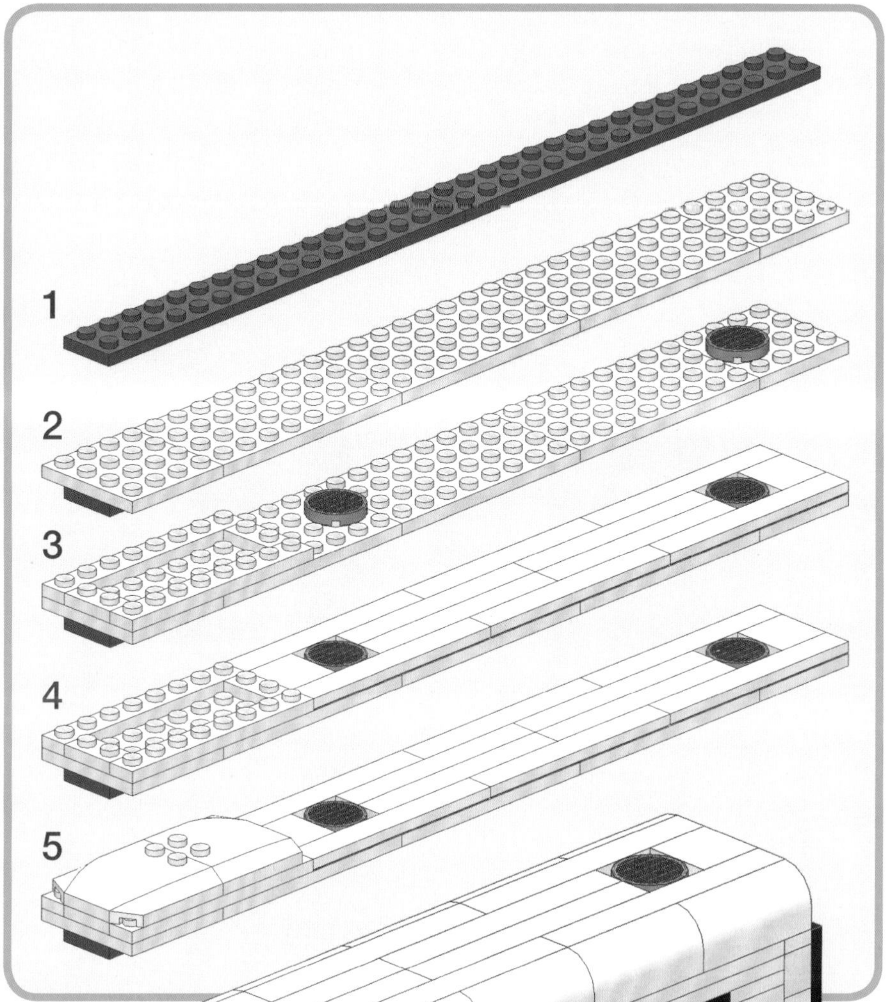

1

2

3

4

5

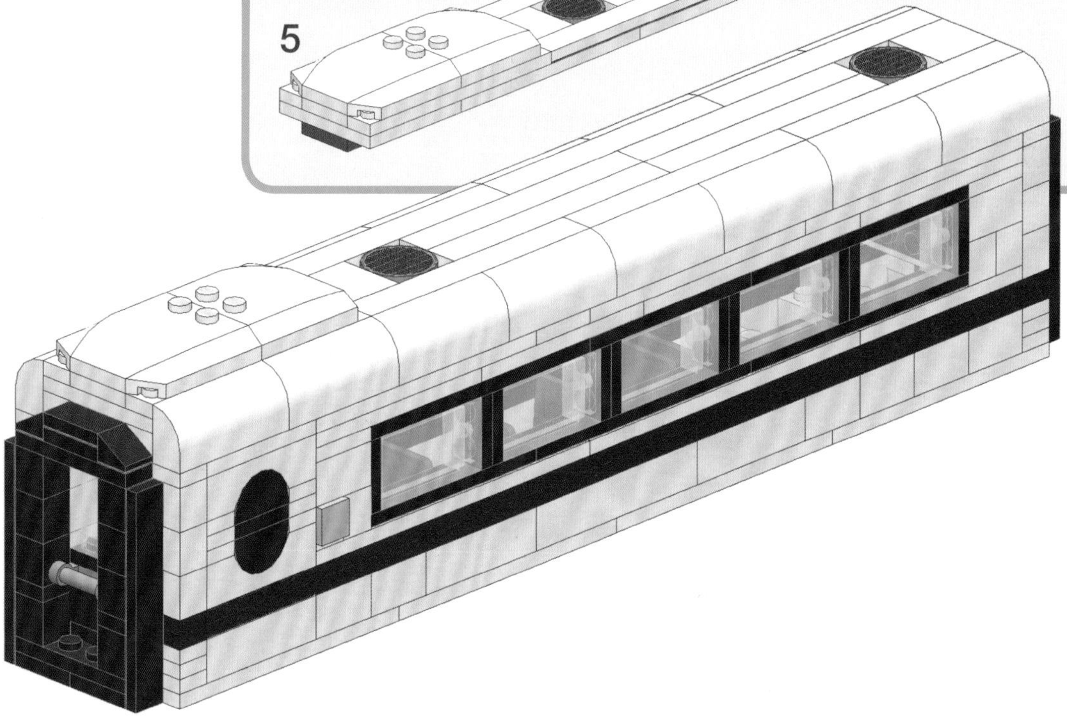

13

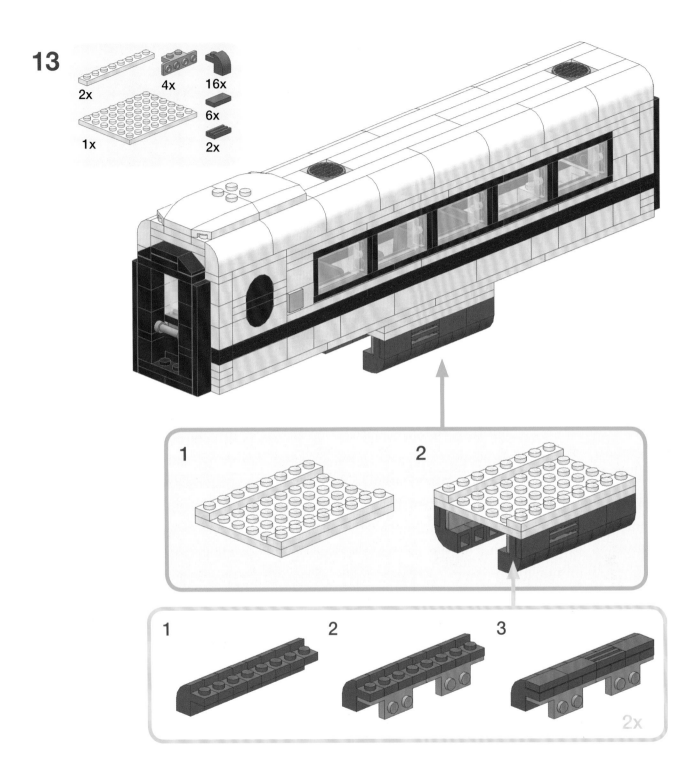

14

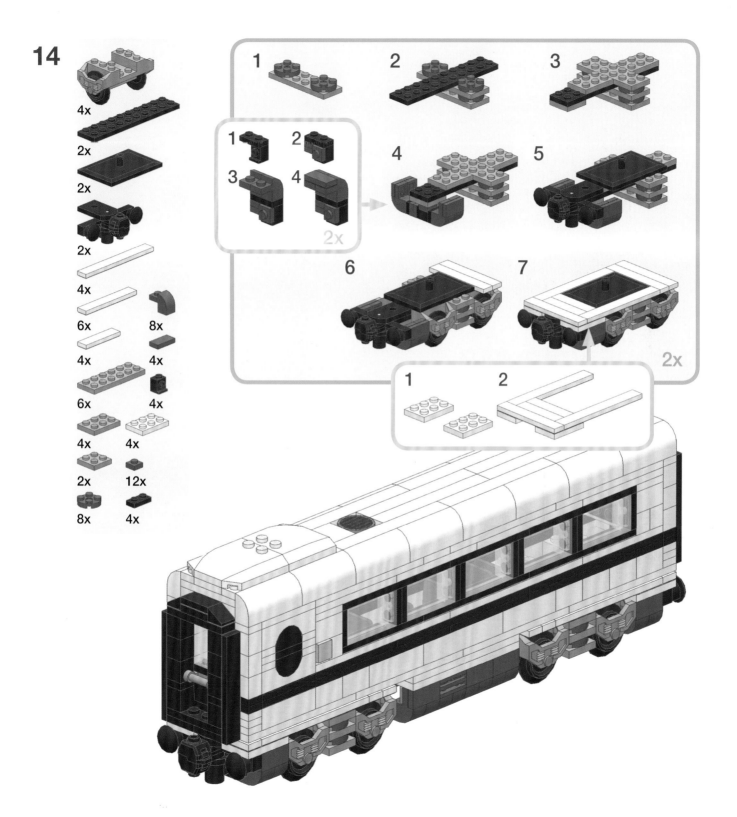

4x
2x
2x
2x
4x
6x 8x
4x 4x
6x 4x
4x 4x
2x 12x
8x 4x

1 2 3

1 2
3 4
2x

4 5

6 7
2x

1 2

ICE 3 DRIVING CAR

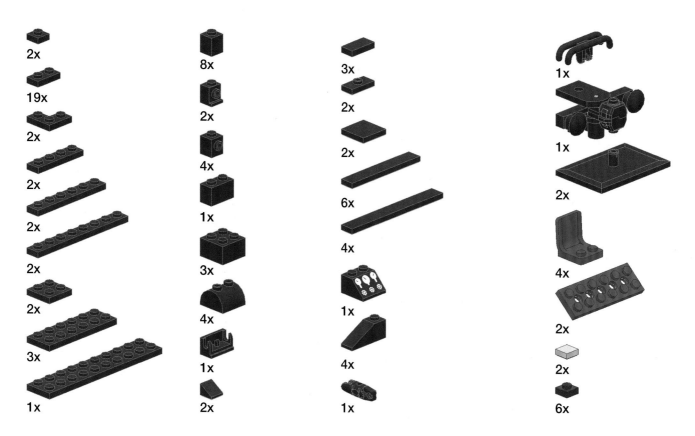

2x

19x

2x

2x

2x

2x

2x

3x

1x

8x

2x

4x

1x

3x

4x

1x

2x

3x

2x

2x

6x

4x

1x

4x

1x

1x

1x

2x

4x

2x

2x

6x

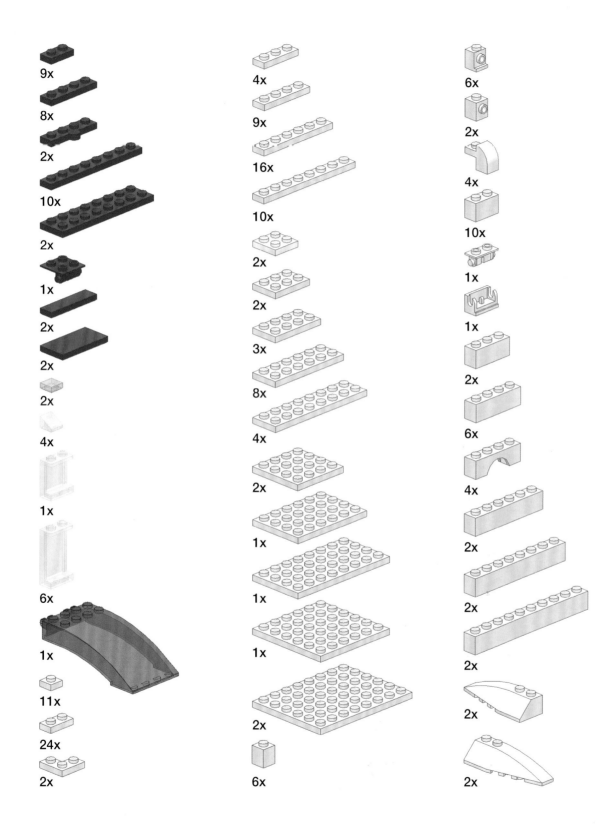

9x

8x

2x

10x

2x

1x

2x

2x

2x

4x

1x

6x

1x

11x

24x

2x

4x

9x

16x

10x

2x

2x

3x

8x

4x

2x

1x

1x

1x

2x

6x

6x

2x

4x

10x

1x

1x

2x

6x

4x

2x

2x

2x

2x

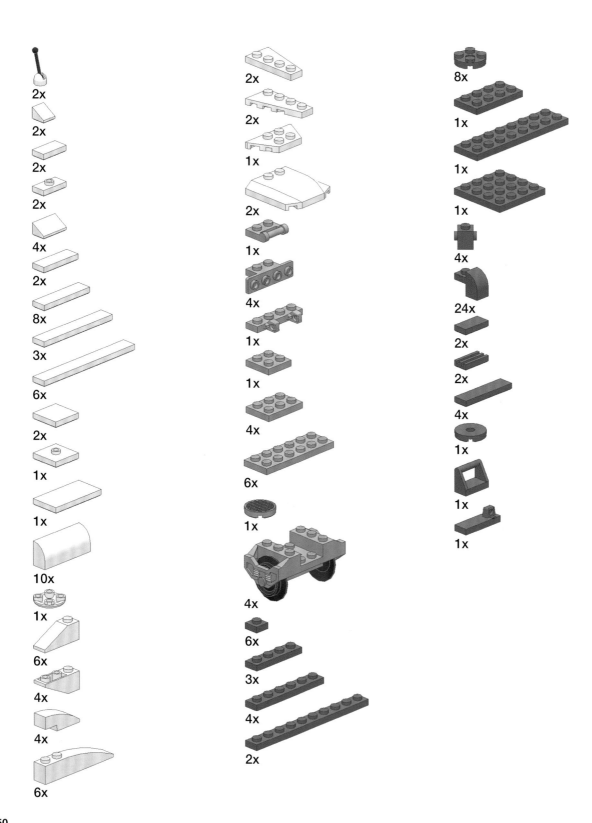

2x

2x

2x

2x

4x

2x

8x

3x

6x

2x

1x

1x

10x

1x

6x

4x

4x

6x

2x

2x

1x

2x

1x

4x

1x

1x

4x

1x

4x

1x

1x

6x

1x

4x

6x

4x

2x

8x

1x

1x

1x

4x

24x

2x

2x

4x

1x

1x

1x

1

1x
1x
4x
2x
2x

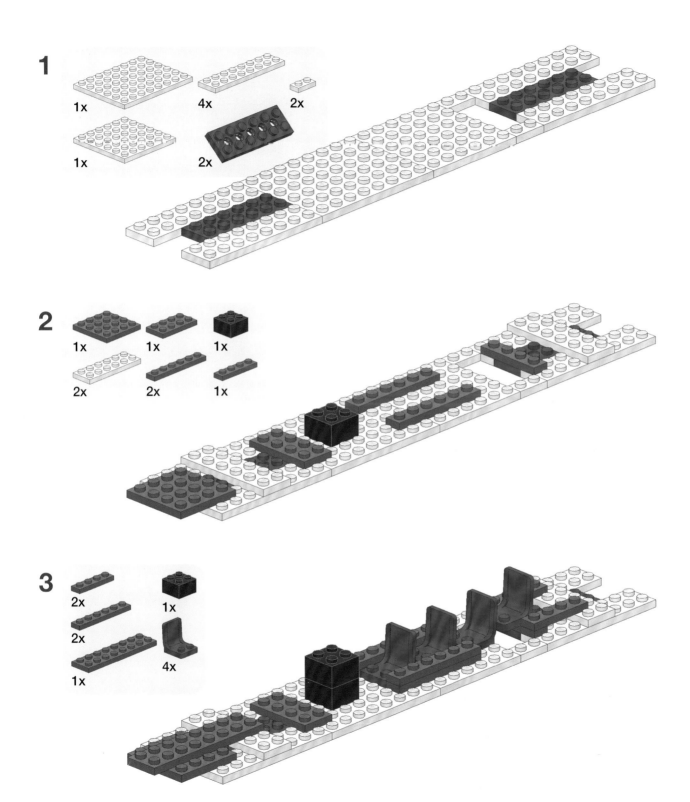

2

1x
1x
1x
2x
2x
1x

3

2x
2x
1x
1x
4x

4

2x 2x 1x
2x 2x
2x 2x

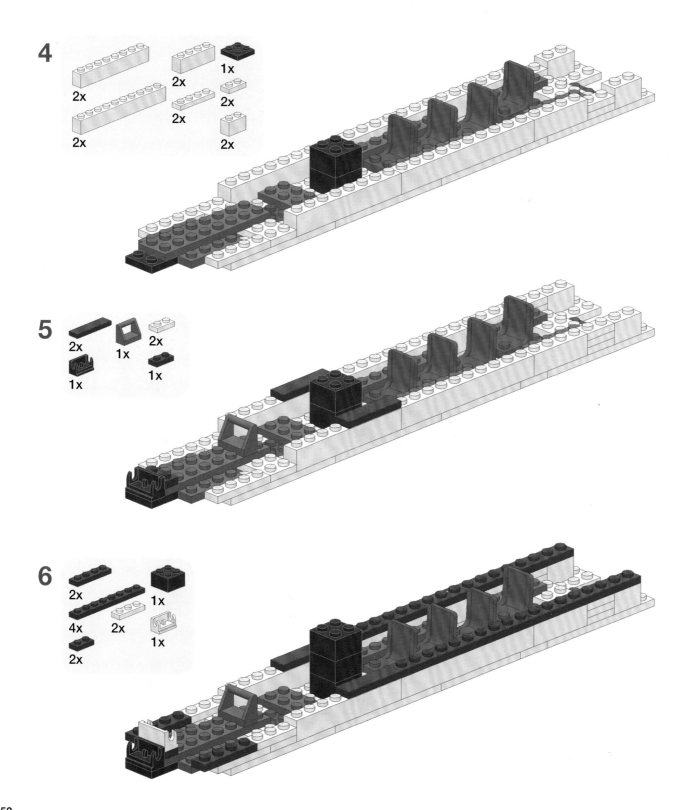

5

2x 1x 2x
1x 1x

6

2x 1x
4x 2x 1x
2x

7

2x 2x
4x 2x 2x

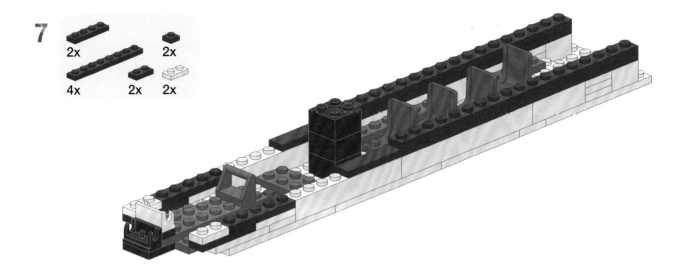

8

2x 2x
4x
1x 2x

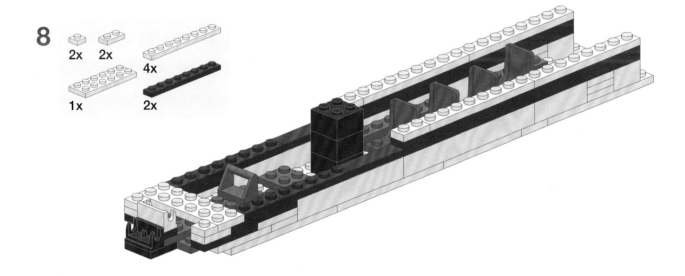

9

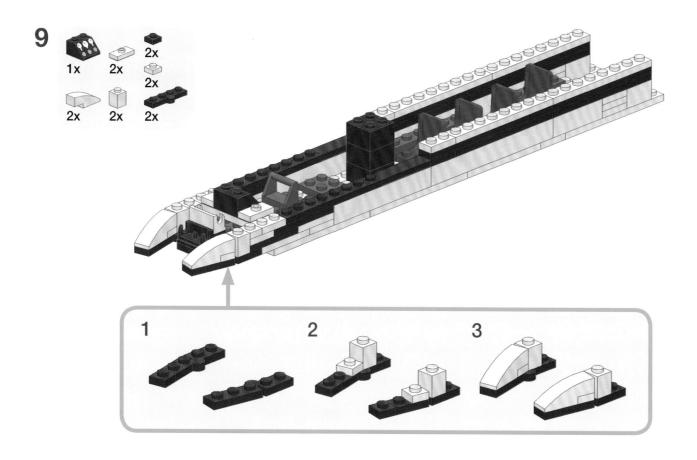

1   2   3

10

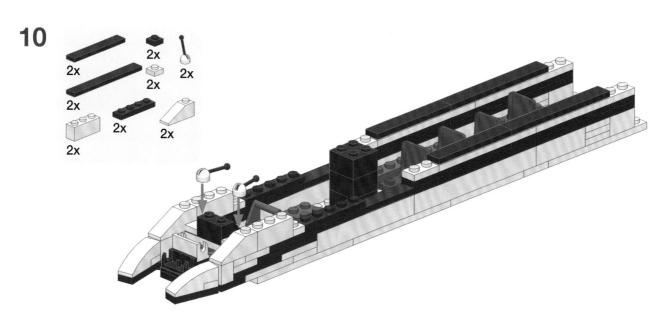

11

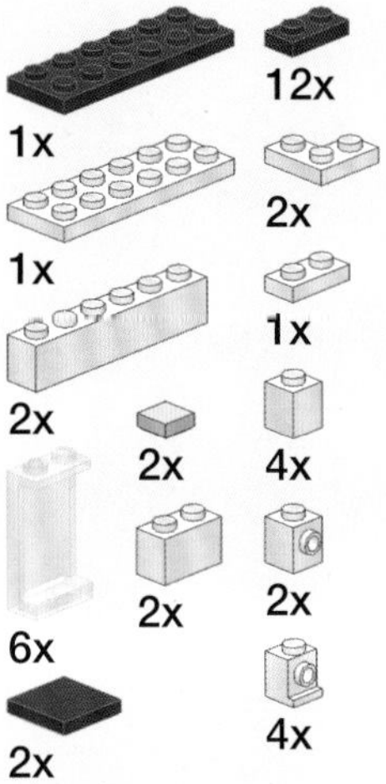
1x
12x
1x
2x
1x
2x
2x
4x
2x
2x
6x
2x
2x
4x

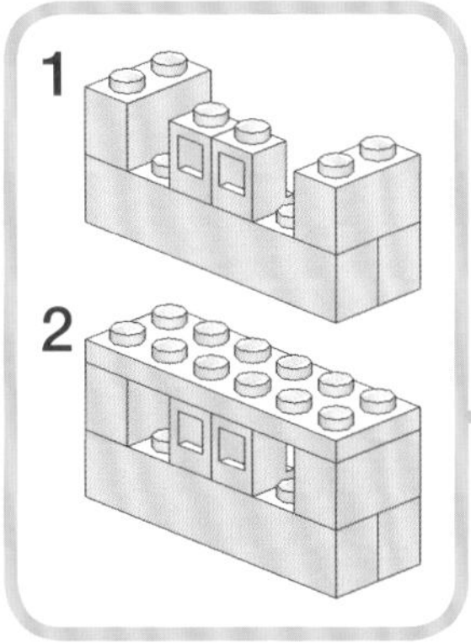
1
2

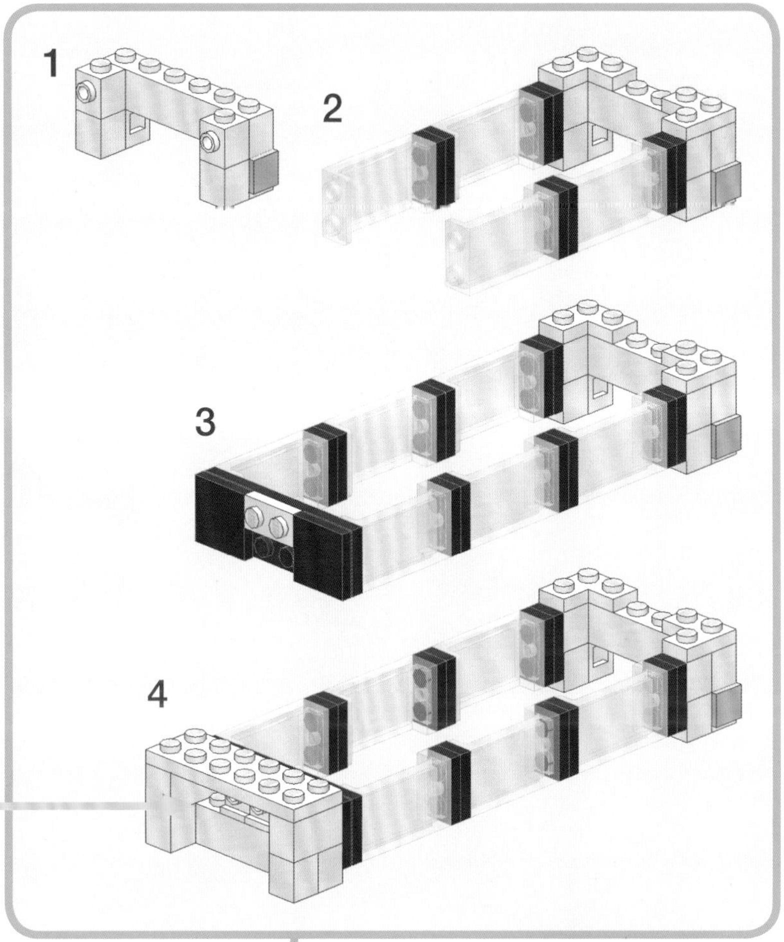
1
2
3
4

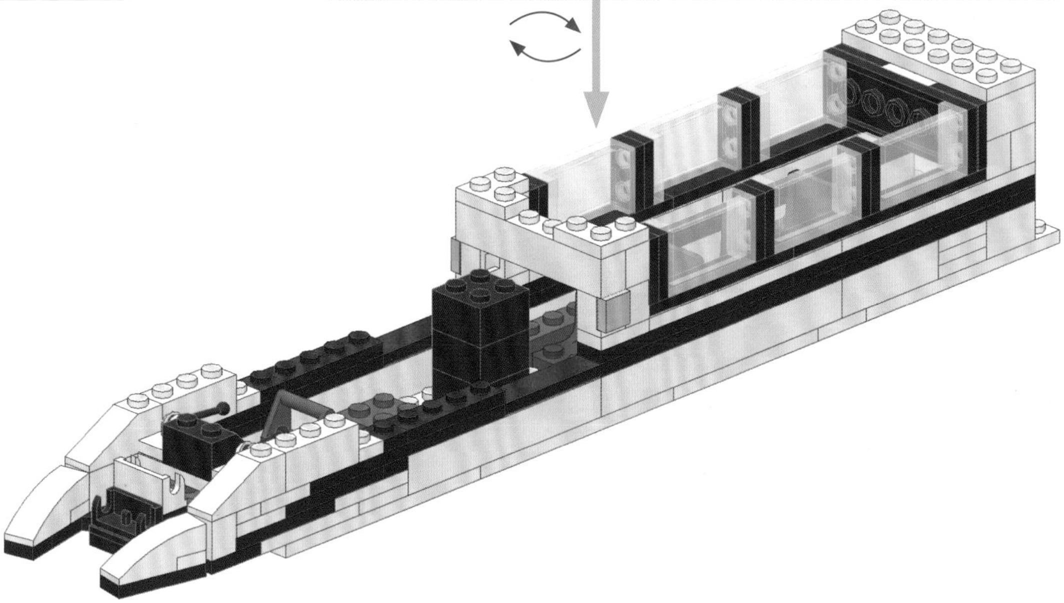

12

2x 2x
2x 2x
2x

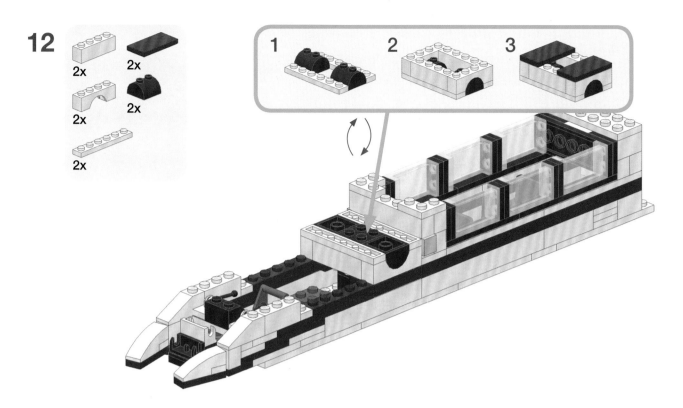

13

4x
2x
1x
2x
1x
2x

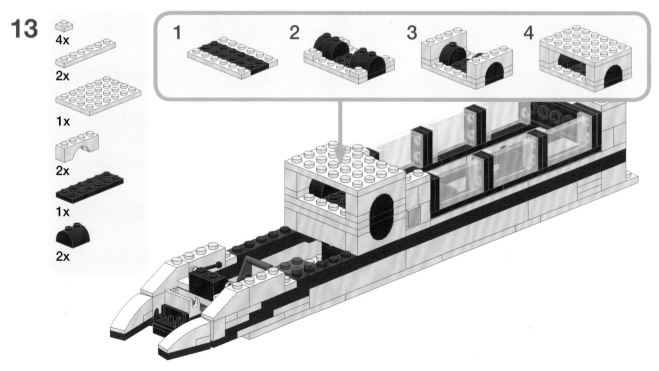

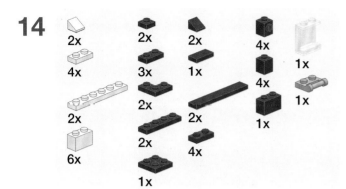

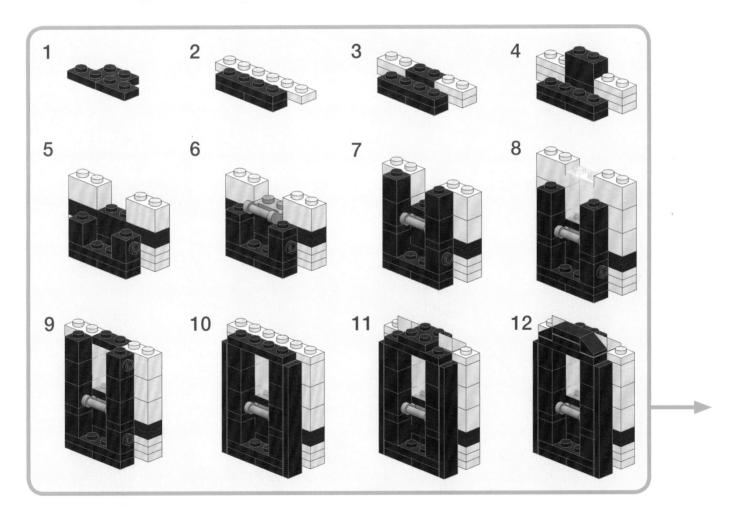

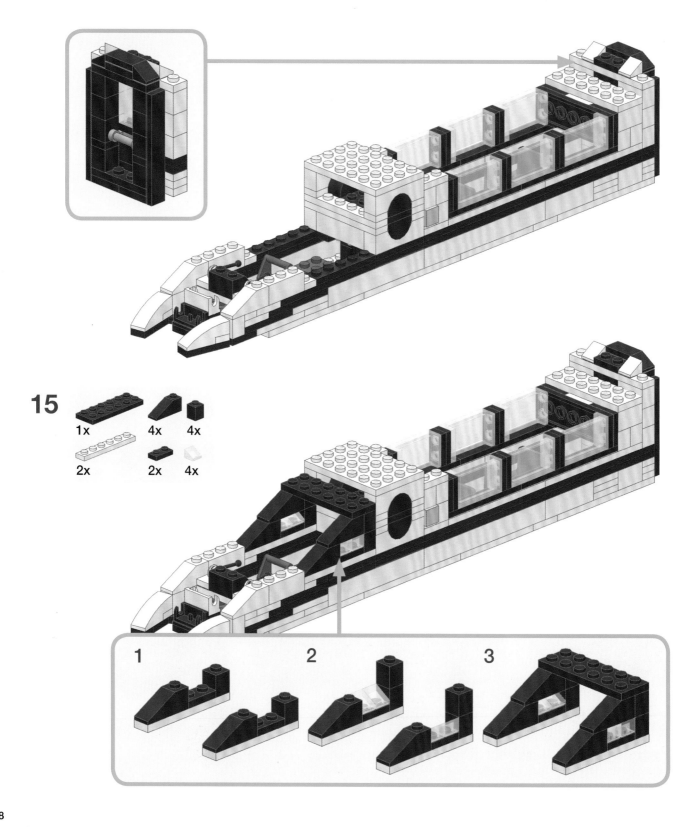

15

1x 4x 4x

2x 2x 4x

1 2 3

16

1x
1x
1x
1x

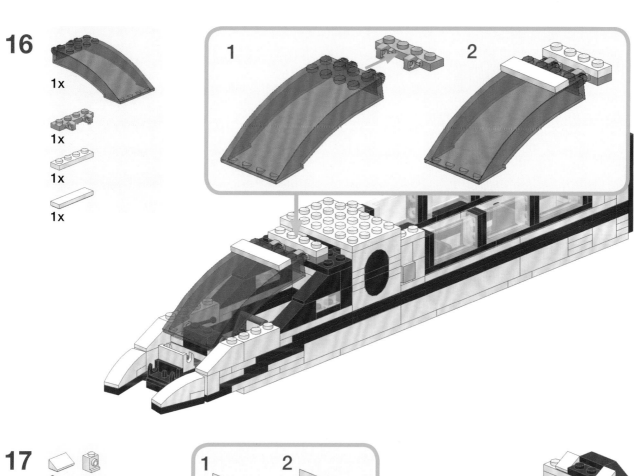

17

2x 2x
1x 2x

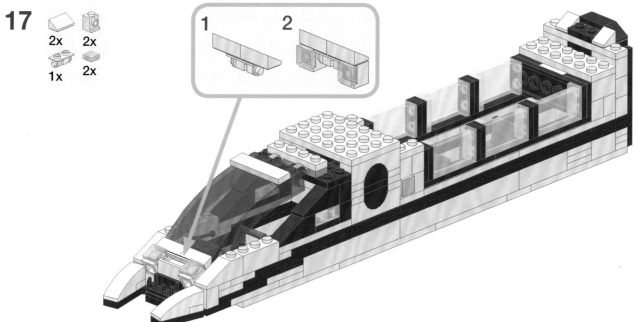

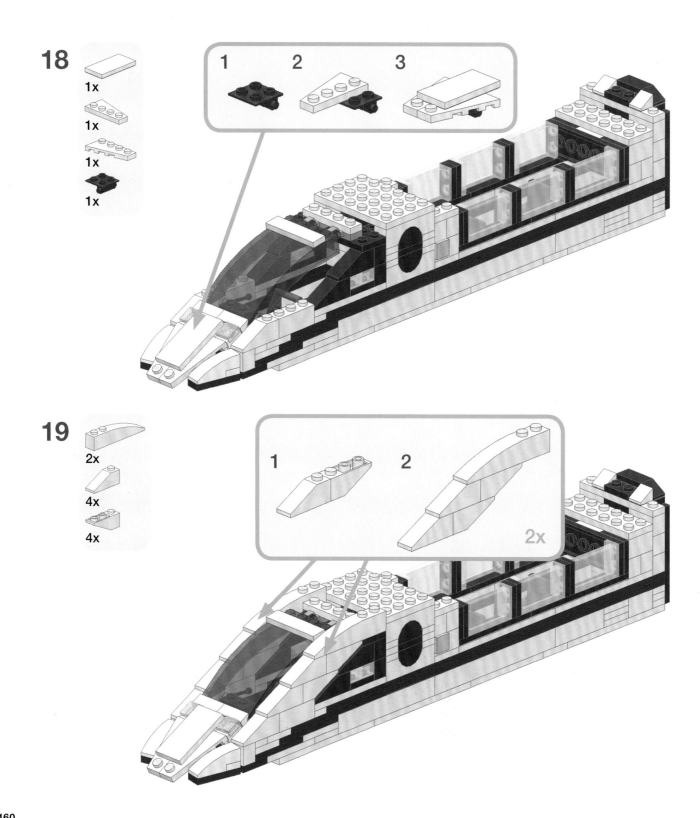

20

1x
1x
2x
2x

1   2   3

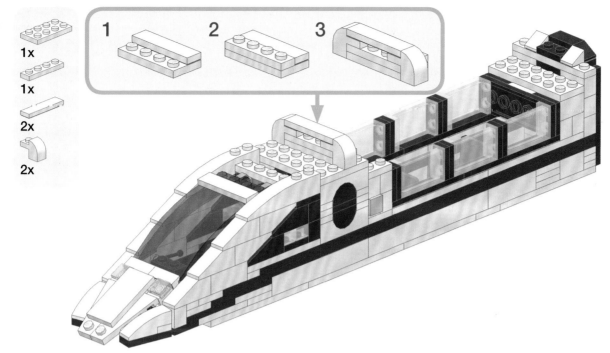

21

1x   1x
2x   1x
1x   1x

1   2

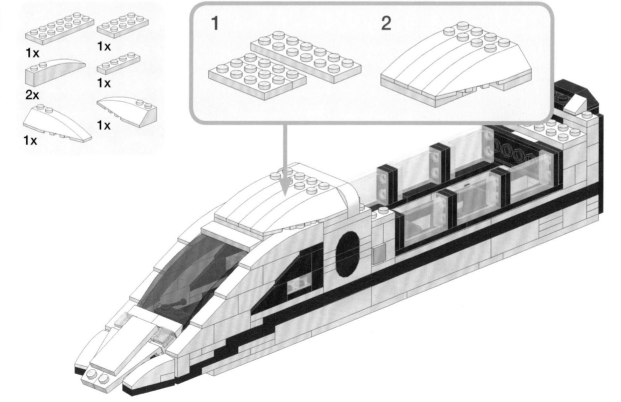

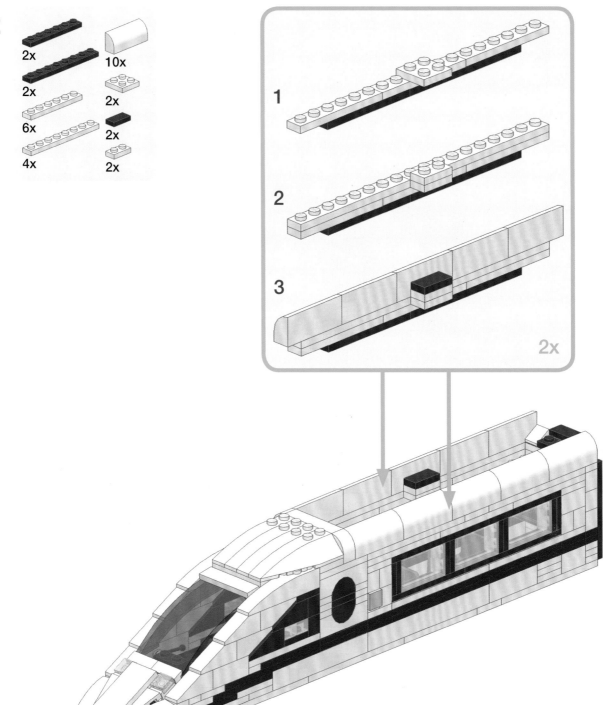

22

2x 10x
2x
6x 2x
4x 2x
2x
2x

1
2
3
2x

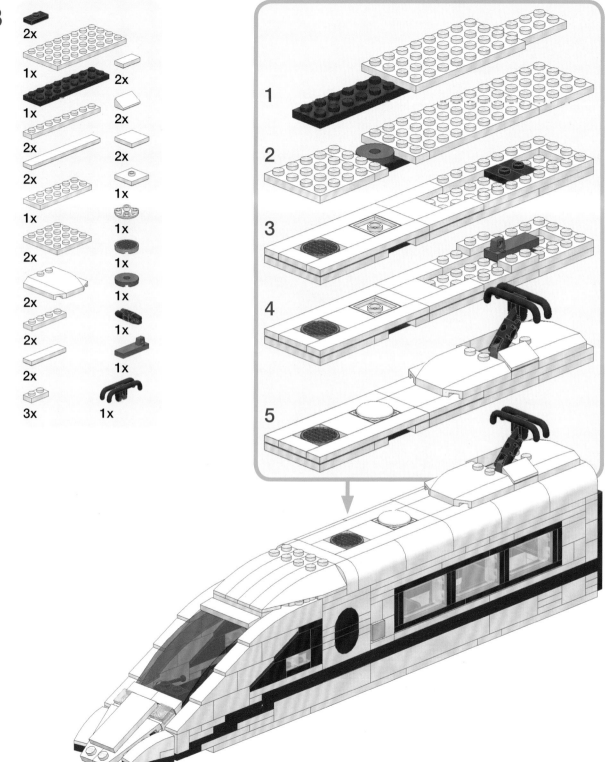

23

2x 1x 2x 1x 2x 2x 2x 1x 2x 2x 2x 2x 3x

2x 2x 1x 1x 1x 1x 1x 1x

1

2

3

4

5

24

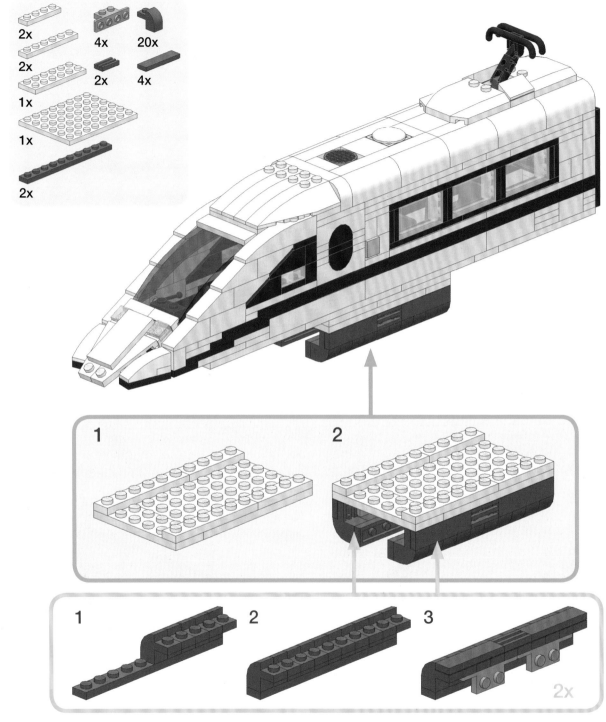

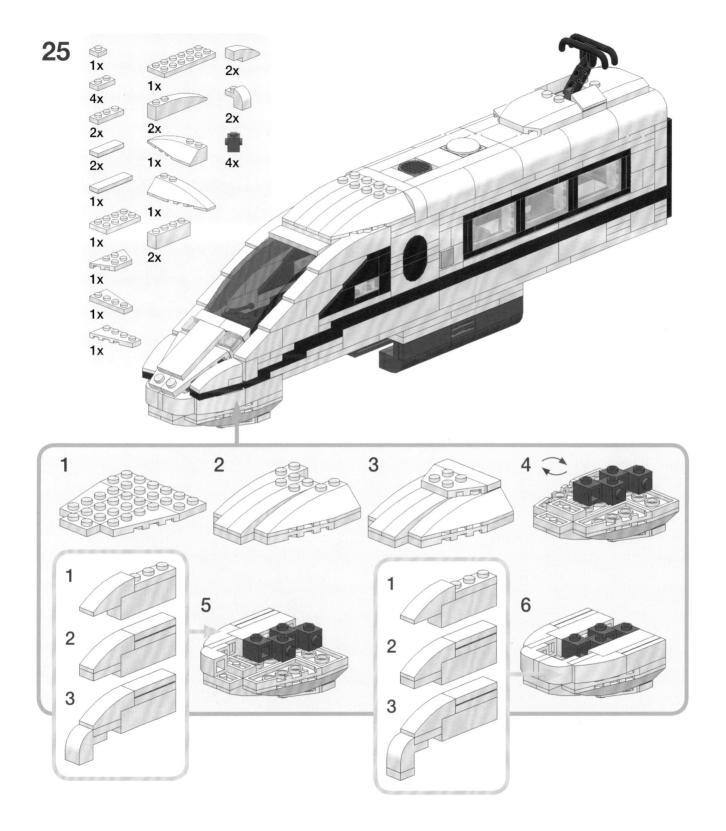

25

1x 4x 2x 2x 1x 1x 1x 1x 1x

1x 2x 1x 1x 2x

2x 2x 4x

1
2
3

1
2
3

4

5

1
2
3

6

26

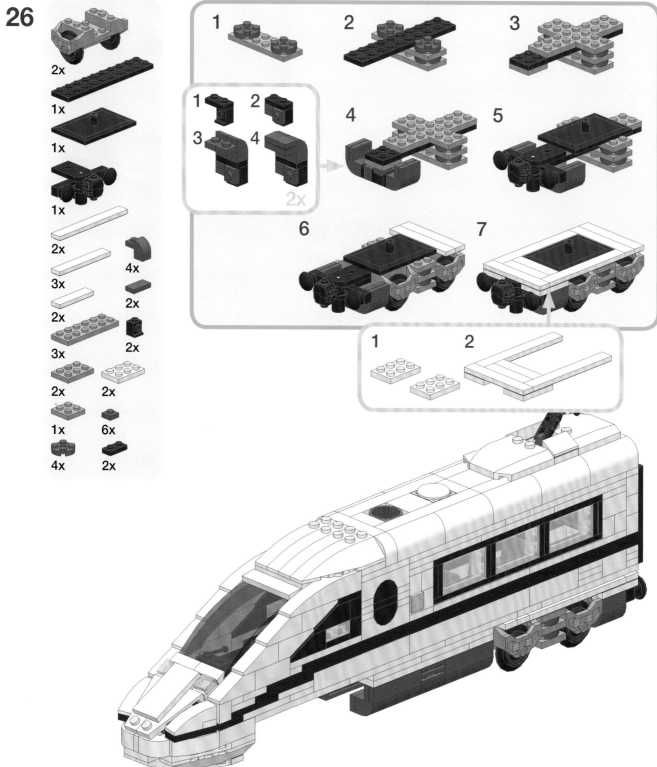

2x
1x
1x
1x
2x
3x
2x
3x
2x 2x
1x 6x
4x 2x

4x
2x
2x

1
2
3

1
2
3
4

2x

4
5

6
7

1
2

27

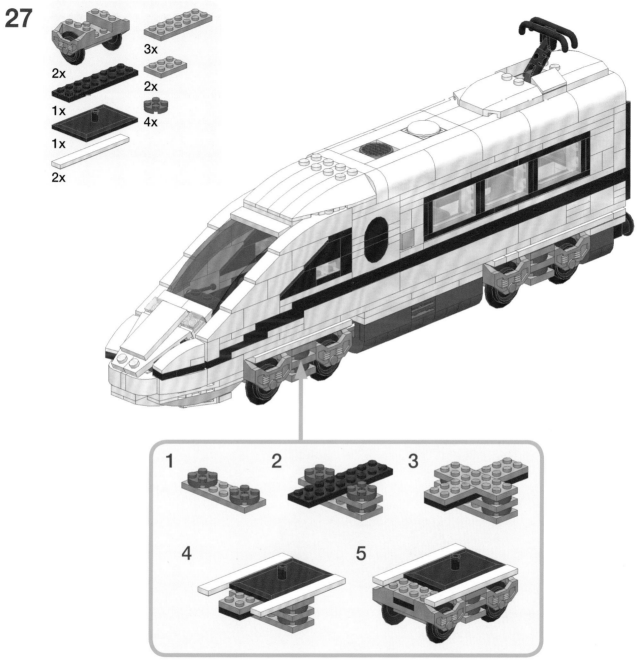

2x
1x
1x
2x
3x
2x
4x

1

2

3

4

5

FITTING THE POWER FUNCTIONS COMPONENTS

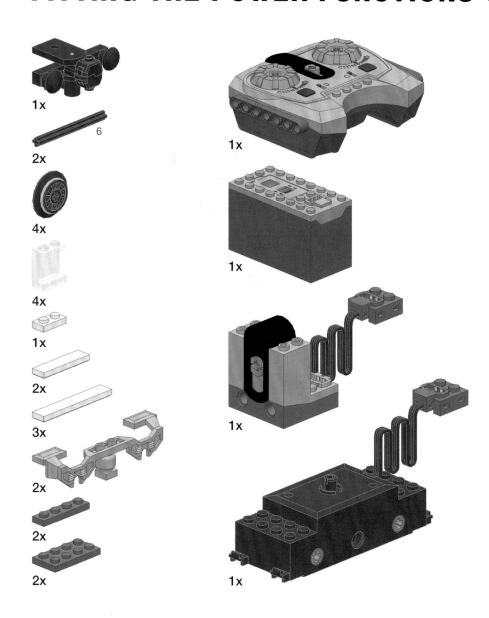

1x

2x 6

4x

4x

1x

2x

3x

2x

2x

2x

1x

1x

1x

1x

1

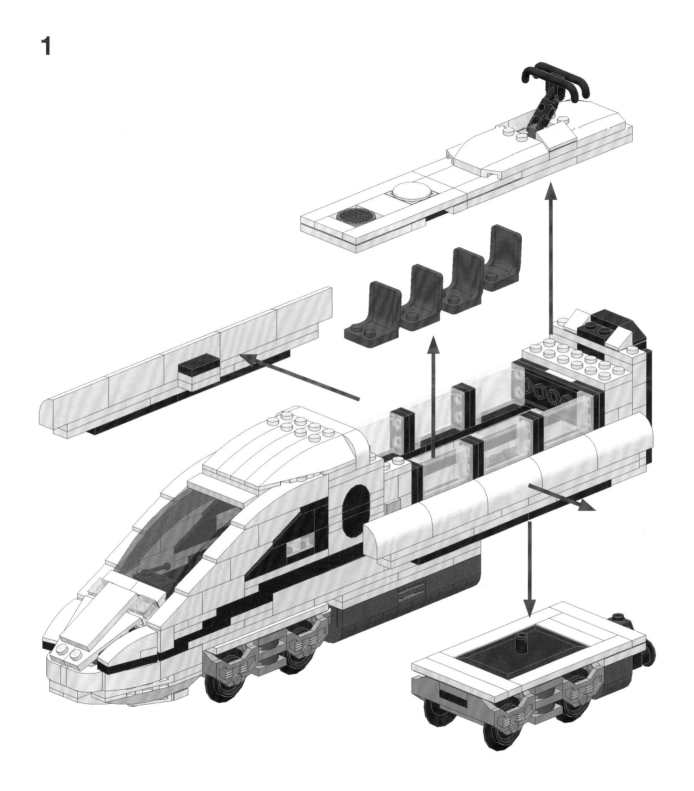

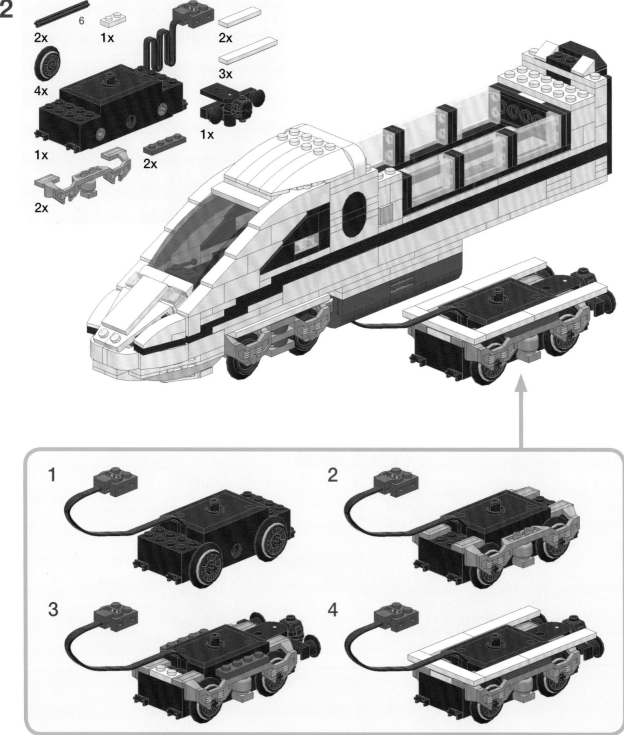

2

2x 6
4x
1x
1x
2x

2x
3x
1x

1

2

3

4

3

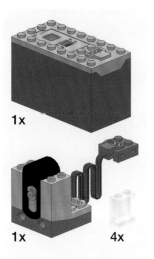

1x

1x   4x

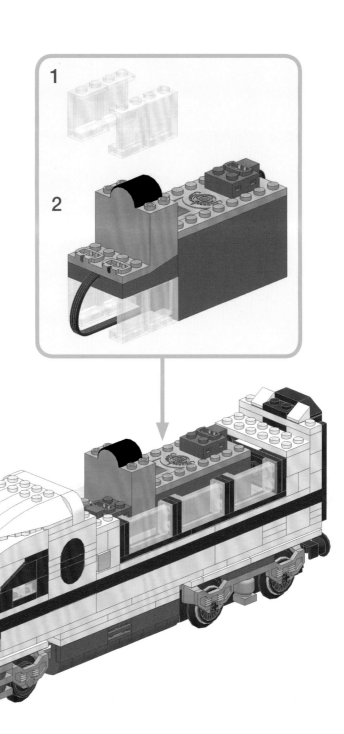

1

2

4

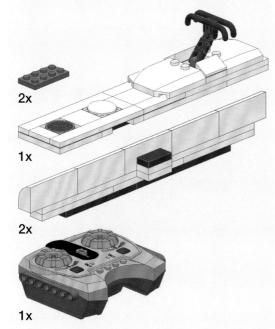

2x

1x

2x

1x

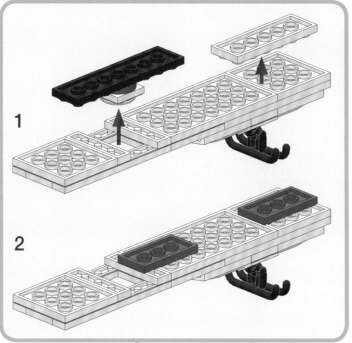

1

2

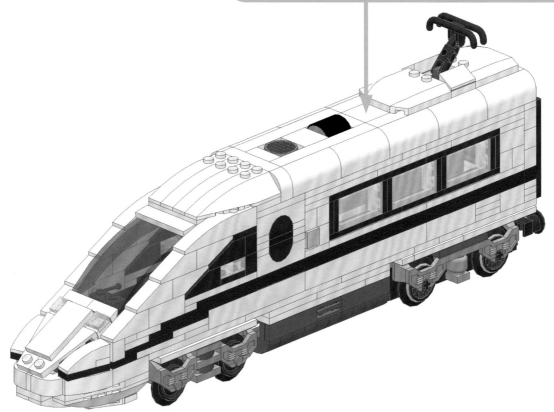

ALTERNATIVE DESIGNS FOR THE WINDSHIELD

WINDSHIELD VARIATION A

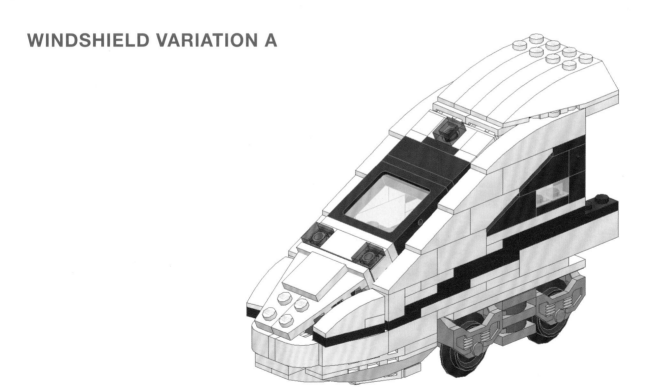

1

1x 1x

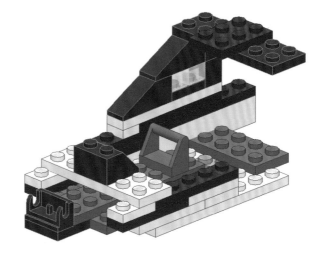

2

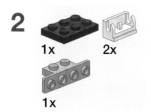

1x 2x

1x

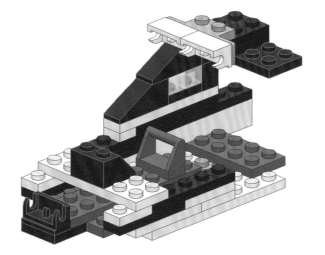

3

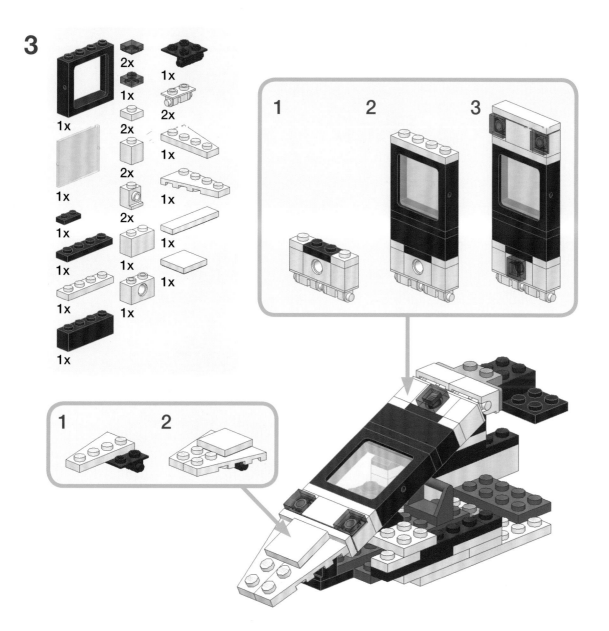

2x
1x
1x
1x
2x
2x
2x
2x

1x
1x
1x
1x
1x
1x
1x

1x
2x
1x
1x
1x

1
2
3

1
2

4

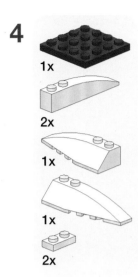

1x

2x

1x

1x

2x

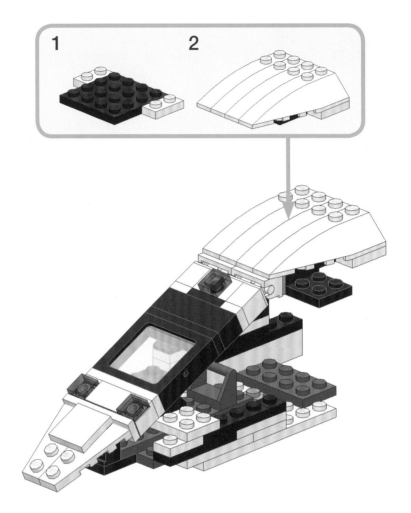

1

2

WINDSHIELD VARIATION B

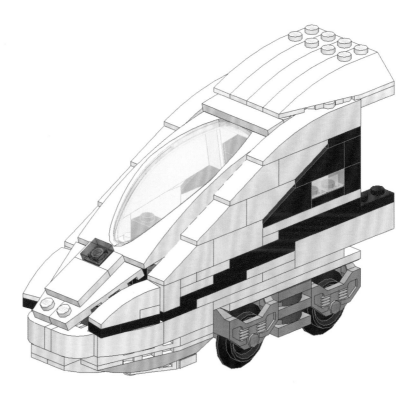

1

1x 1x 2x

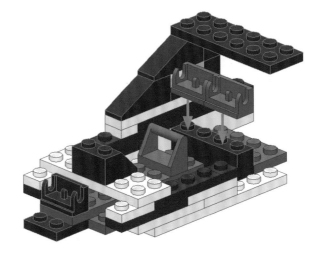

2

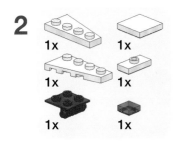

1x 1x

1x 1x

1x 1x

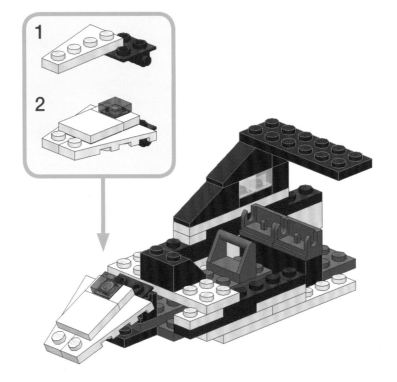

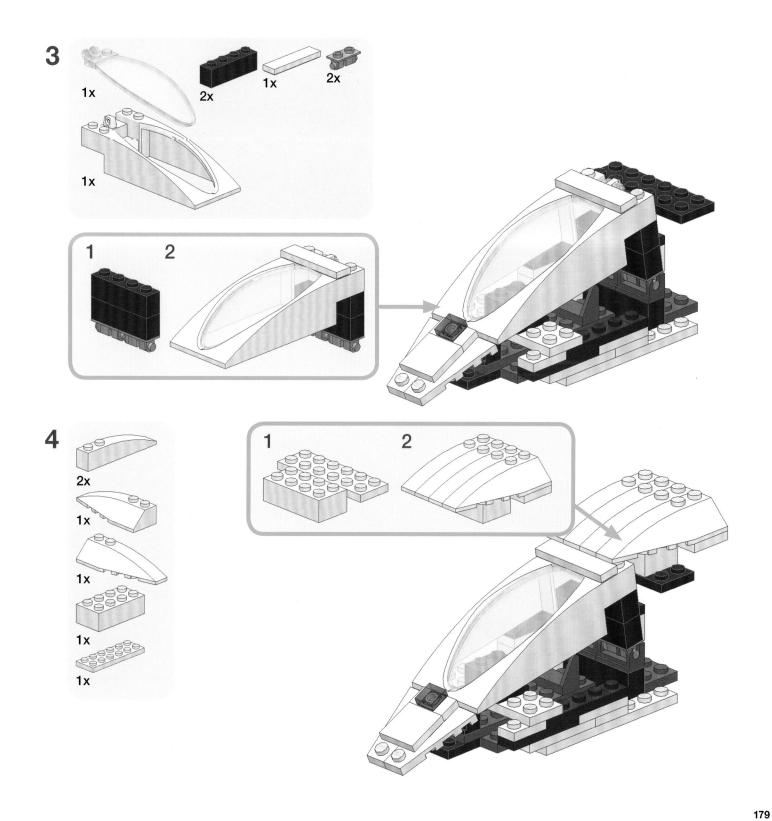

3

1x
2x
1x
2x
1x
1x

1   2

4

2x
1x
1x
1x
1x

1   2

A SIMPLE GONDOLA

You can build this simple but handsome gondola in a number of colors—for example, in light gray, dark gray, brown, or red. You could also make it longer and put it on trucks.

For the cargo, you could use small parts like 1×1 plates in gray and brown to represent scrap metal.

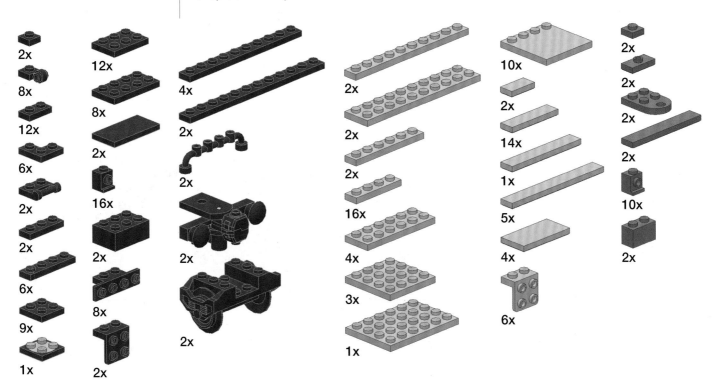

2x

8x

12x

6x

2x

2x

6x

9x

1x

12x

8x

2x

16x

2x

8x

2x

4x

2x

2x

2x

2x

2x

2x

2x

2x

2x

16x

4x

3x

1x

10x

2x

14x

1x

5x

4x

6x

2x

2x

2x

2x

10x

2x

1

1x

1x   1x

2

2x

3

2x   3x

4x

4

8x

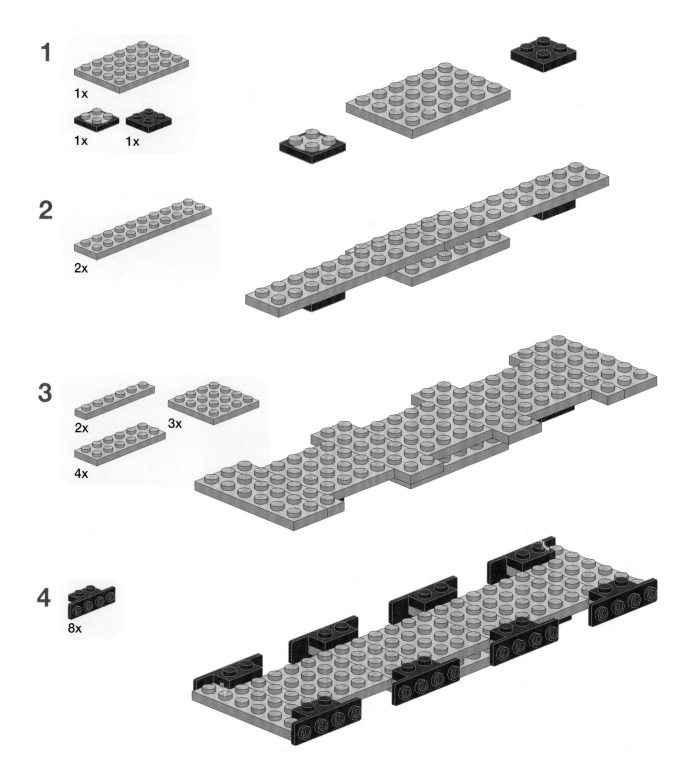

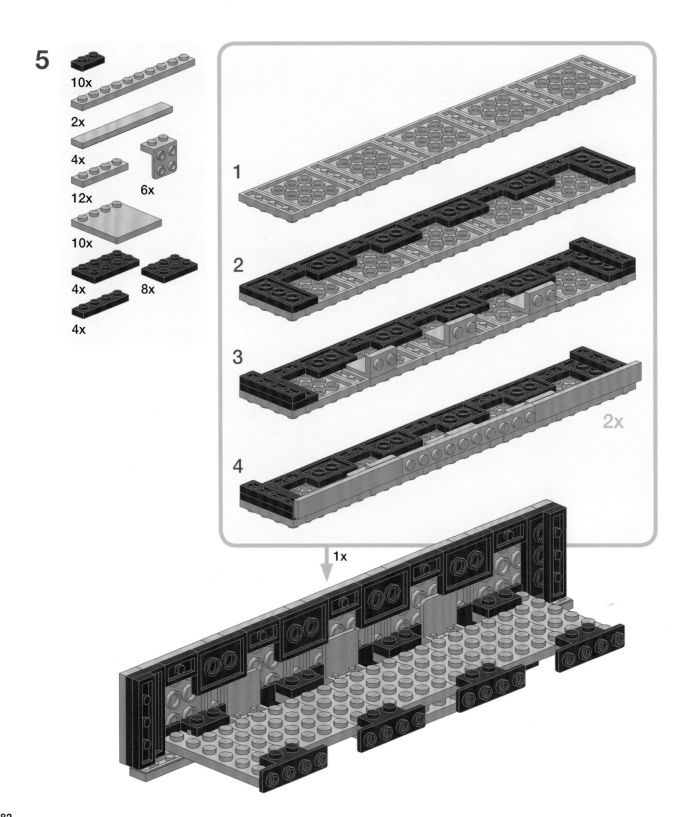

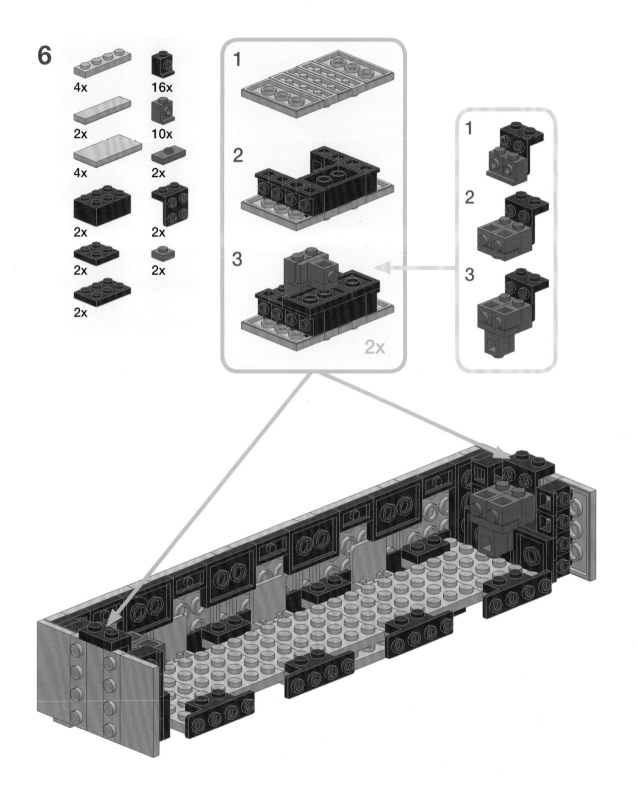

6

4x
16x
2x
10x
4x
2x
2x
2x
2x
2x
2x
2x

1

2

3

2x

1

2

3

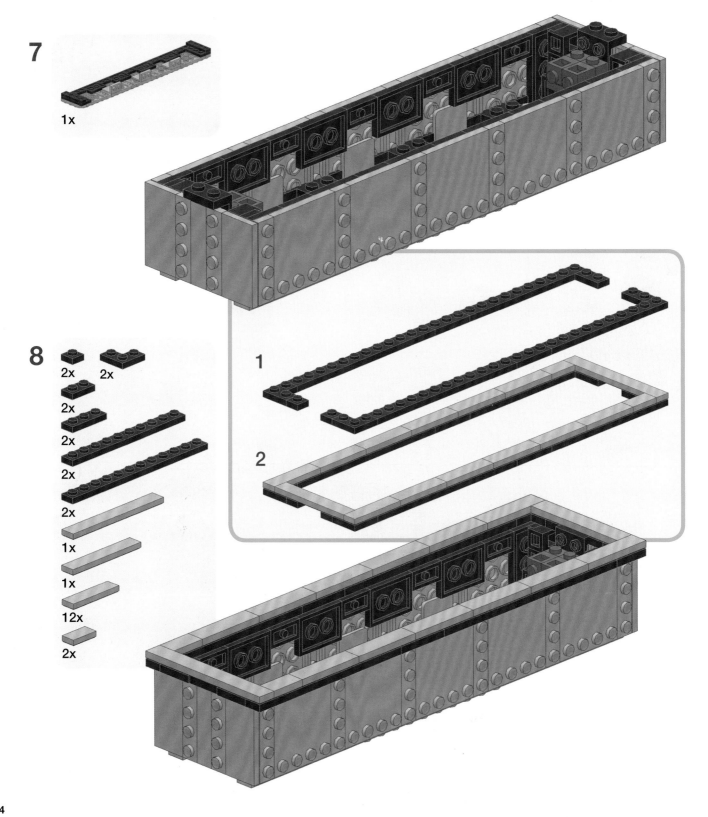

7

1x

8

2x 2x

2x

2x

2x

2x

1x

1x

12x

2x

1

2

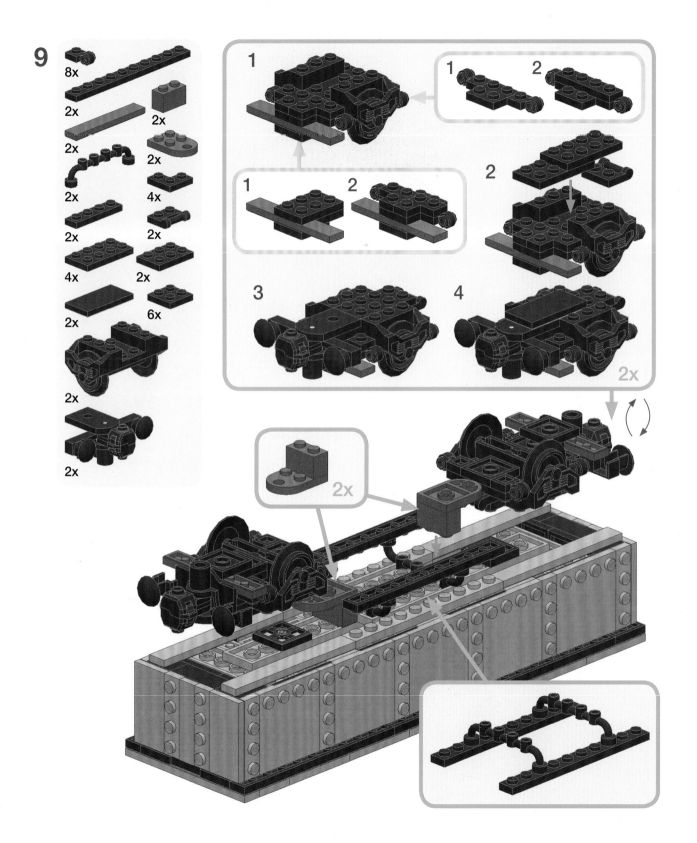

9

8x

2x

2x

2x

2x

2x

4x

2x

4x

2x

2x

6x

2x

2x

1

1   2

1   2

2

3   4

2x

2x

2x

SWISS ELECTRIC LOCOMOTIVE BE 6/8 "CROCODILE"

FACT SHEET

Inspiration: Creating a model of the legendary Swiss Be 6/8 "Crocodile"

Difficulty level: Hard

Style: 7-wide

Drive: Two Power Functions motors, size M

Notes:

- The original train has appeared in brown livery, but dark green would have been my preference for the model. However, parts availability limited this design to brown, and there are still a fair number of rare and expensive pieces. You need four Big Ben Bricks wheels, size medium, with flanges.

- This locomotive is made up of a number of sections that are assembled individually. Because motor cables are routed into the middle section, you need to join the three main sections early on. After that, you'll add the remaining body parts.

- Connect one of the motor cables to the receiver with an extension cable. Pay attention to the color coding of the cables in the instructions.

- You can add a washer to the pivot axle to improve how the leading and trailing axles run. I use a Technic Bush 1/2 Toothed (4265a/4265b), but first I file down its teeth.

To make the instructions easier to follow, all the brown parts have been drawn in red.

Swiss Be 6/8 "Crocodile"

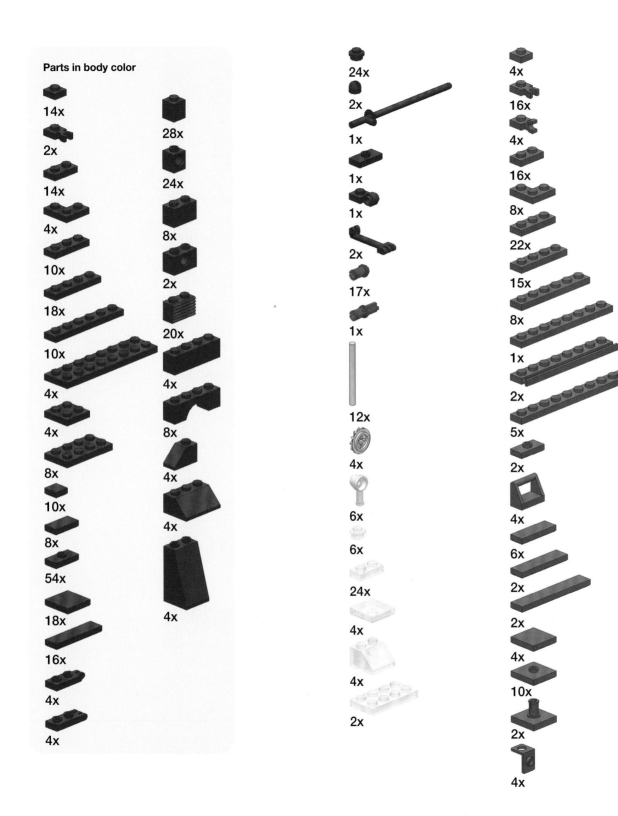

Parts in body color

14x
2x
14x
4x
10x
18x
10x
4x
4x
8x
10x
8x
54x
18x
16x
4x
4x

28x
24x
8x
2x
20x
4x
8x
4x
4x
4x

24x
2x
1x
1x
1x
2x
17x
1x
12x
4x
6x
6x
24x
4x
4x
4x
2x

4x
16x
4x
16x
8x
22x
15x
8x
1x
2x
5x
2x
4x
6x
2x
2x
4x
10x
2x
4x

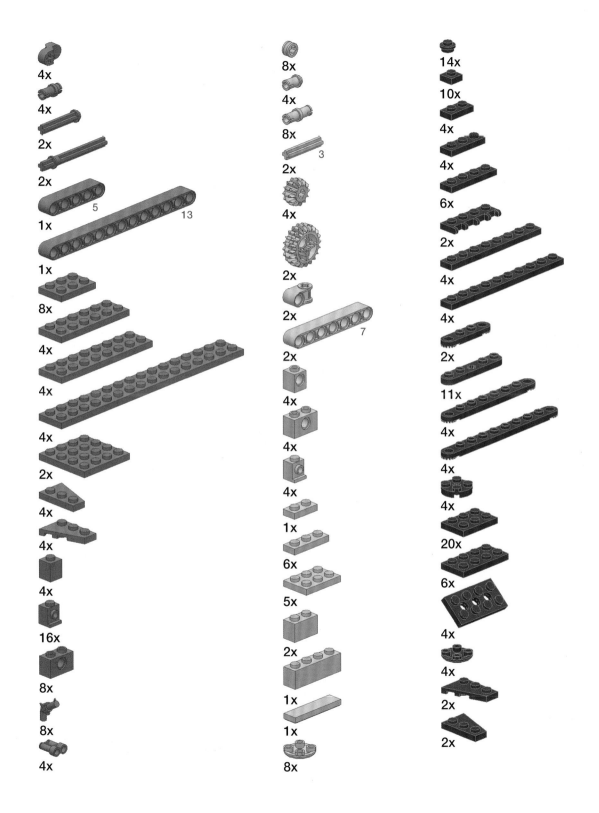

4x

4x

2x

2x

5

1x

13

1x

8x

4x

4x

4x

2x

4x

4x

4x

16x

8x

8x

4x

8x

4x

8x

3

2x

4x

2x

2x

2x

7

2x

4x

4x

4x

1x

6x

5x

2x

1x

1x

8x

14x

10x

4x

4x

6x

2x

4x

4x

2x

11x

4x

4x

4x

20x

6x

4x

4x

2x

2x

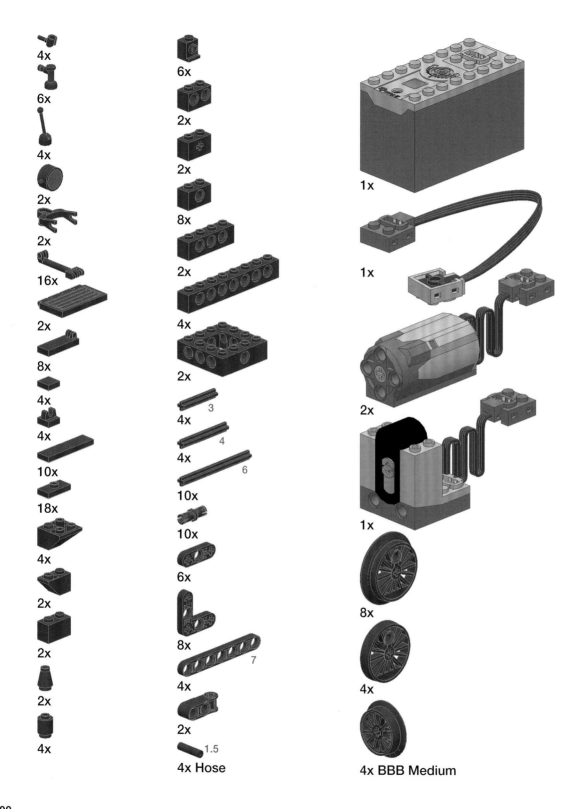

4x

6x

4x

2x

2x

16x

2x

8x

4x

4x

10x

18x

4x

2x

2x

2x

4x

6x

2x

2x

2x

8x

2x

4x

2x

8x

2x

4x

4x

4x

10x

10x

6x

8x

4x

2x

3

4

6

7

1.5

4x Hose

1x

1x

2x

1x

8x

4x

4x BBB Medium

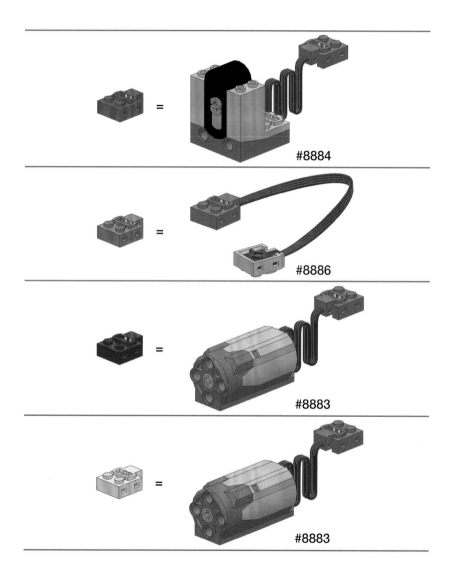

= #8884

= #8886

= #8883

= #8883

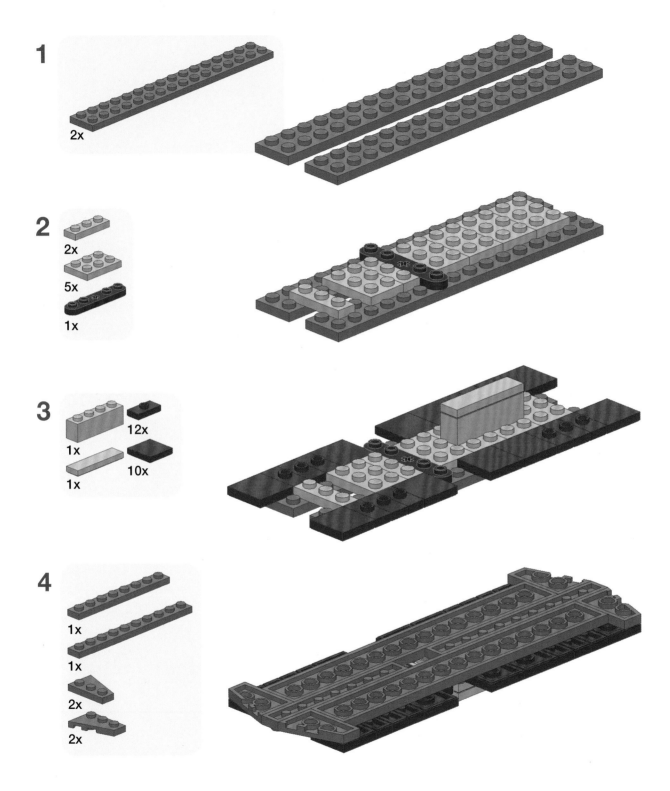

1

2x

2

2x

5x

1x

3

1x

12x

1x

10x

4

1x

1x

2x

2x

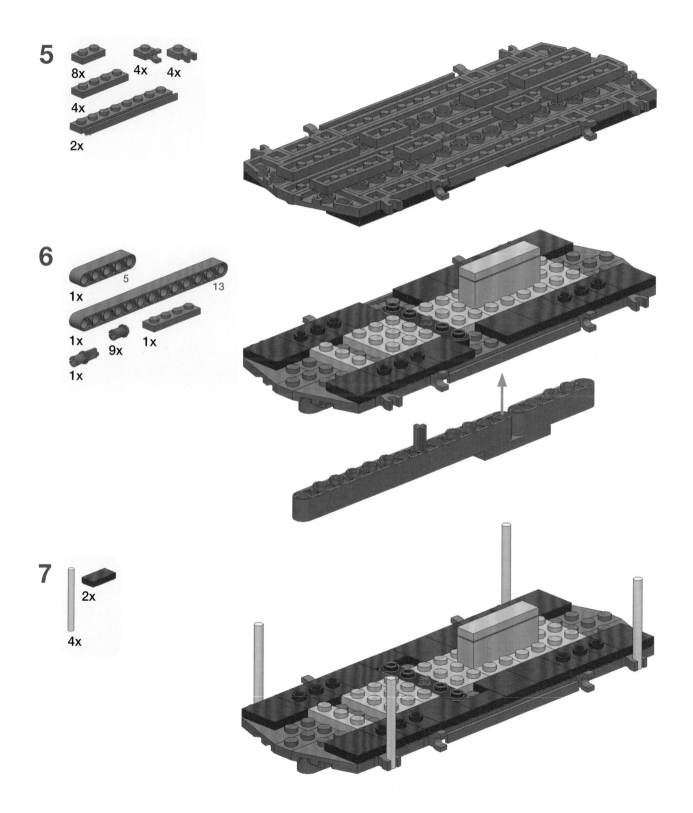

8

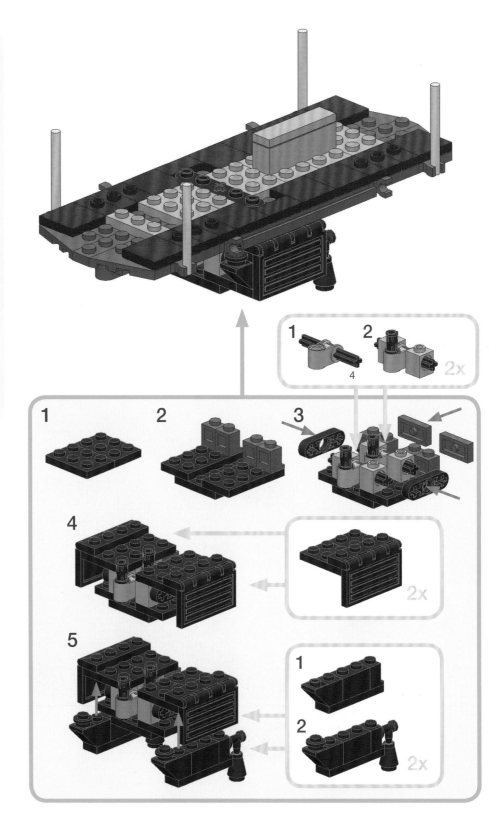

9

2x 2x

2x

2x

2x

2x

10

1x

1x

11

1x

1x

12

1x

2x

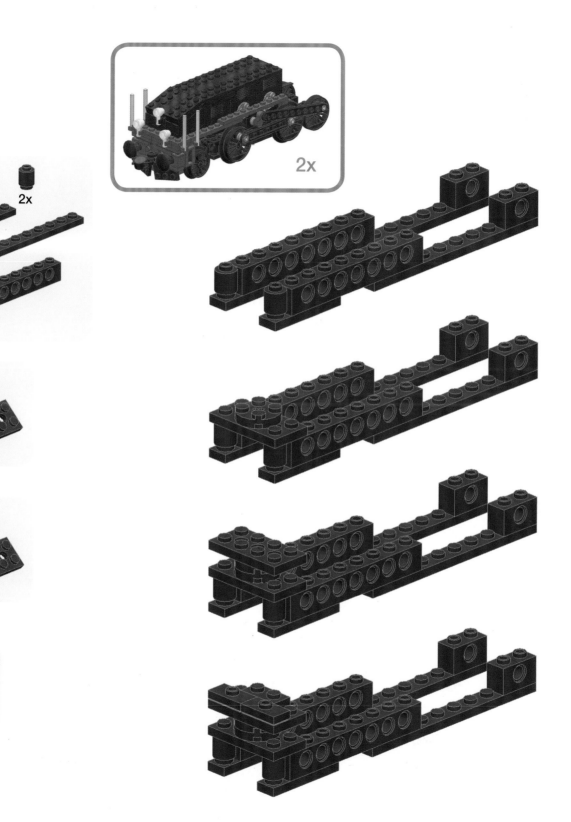

13

1x
1x

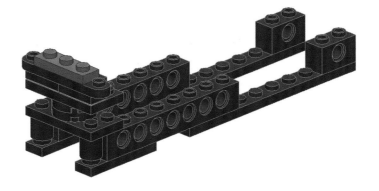

14

4x
2x
2x
1x
1x
1x
2x
2x
1x
1x
1x
1x
2x
1x
1x
2x
1x
6
3

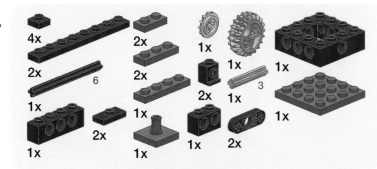

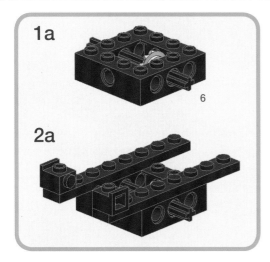

1a
2a
6

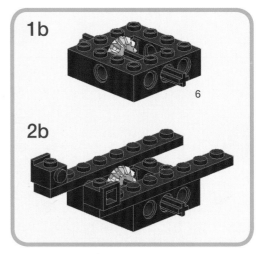

1b
2b
6

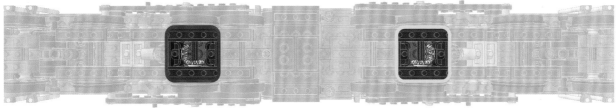

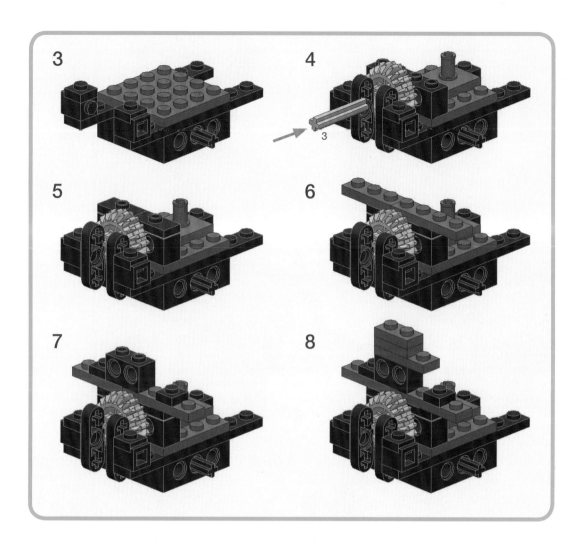

15

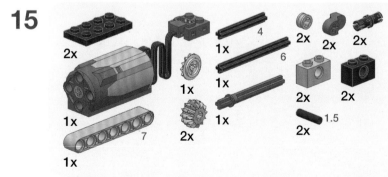

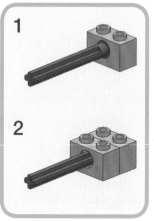

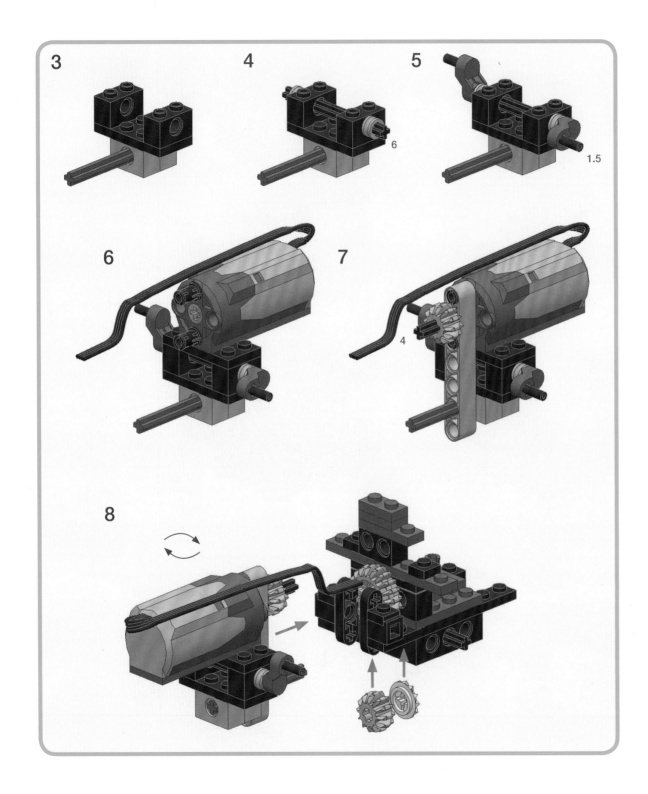

16

2x 6

1x

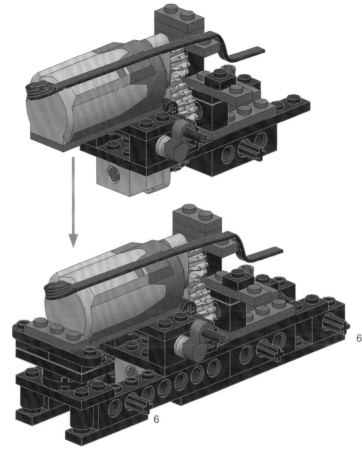

6

6

17

4x 2x

2x 4x

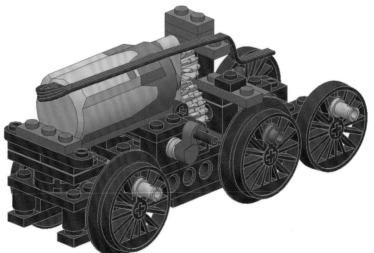

18

2x 2x

7

2x

2x

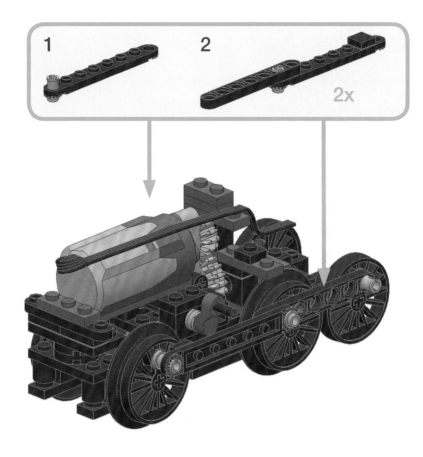

1

2

2x

19

2x

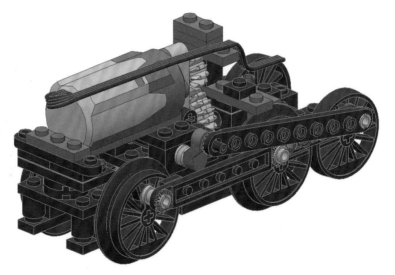

20

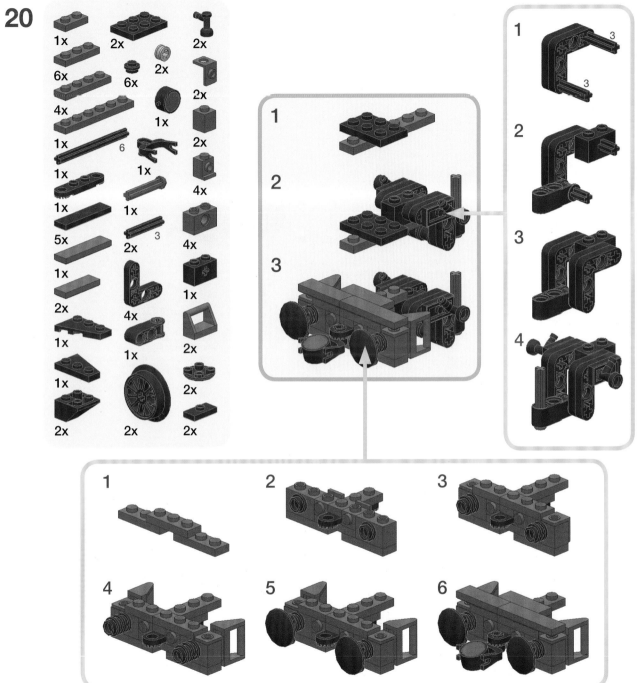

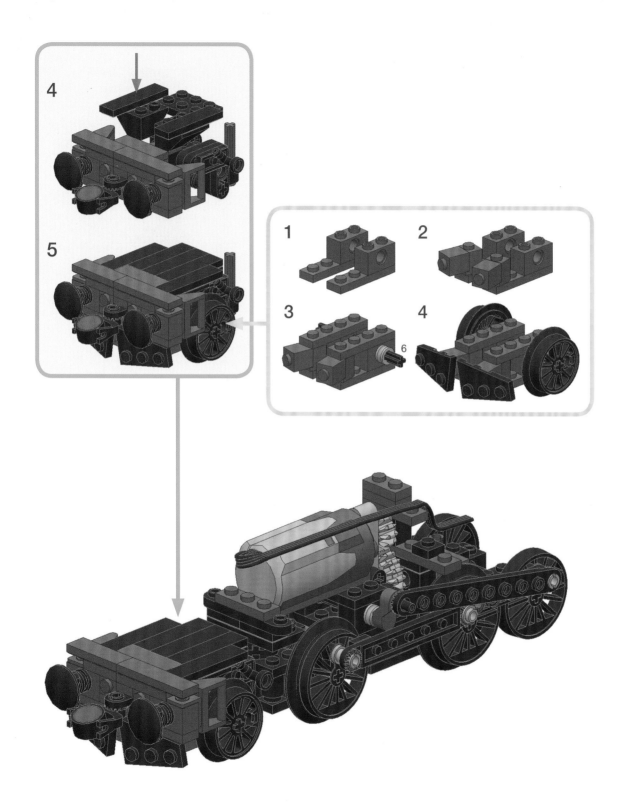

21

1x　2x　2x　4x

22

2x　1x　2x
2x　2x

23

2x　2x　4x
2x
2x　1x　1x

24

4x　2x
2x　2x
4x　2x

25

2x
2x

2x

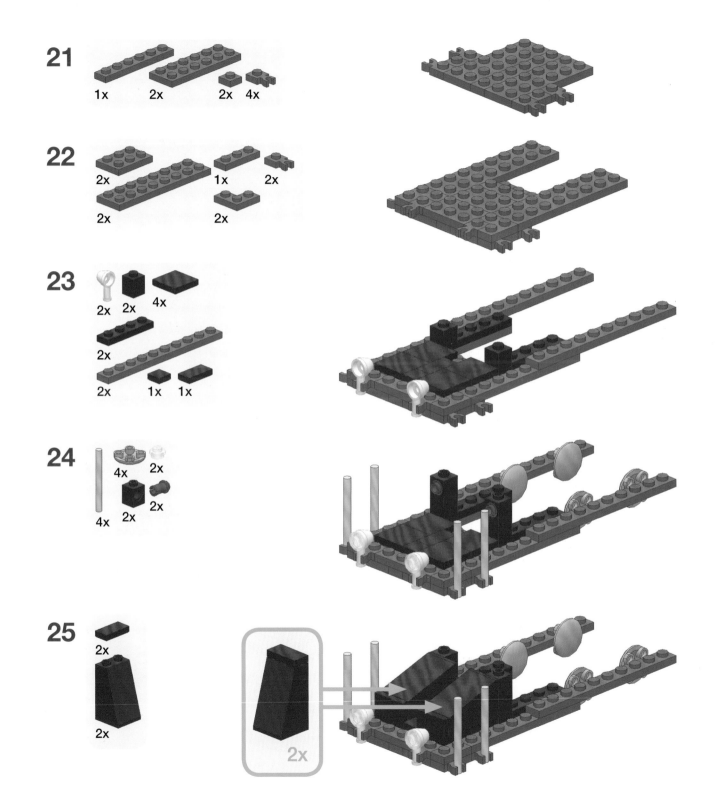

26

2x
2x
2x
4x

27

2x 6x 2x

28

2x
2x
2x

29

2x 2x 3x 1x 4x

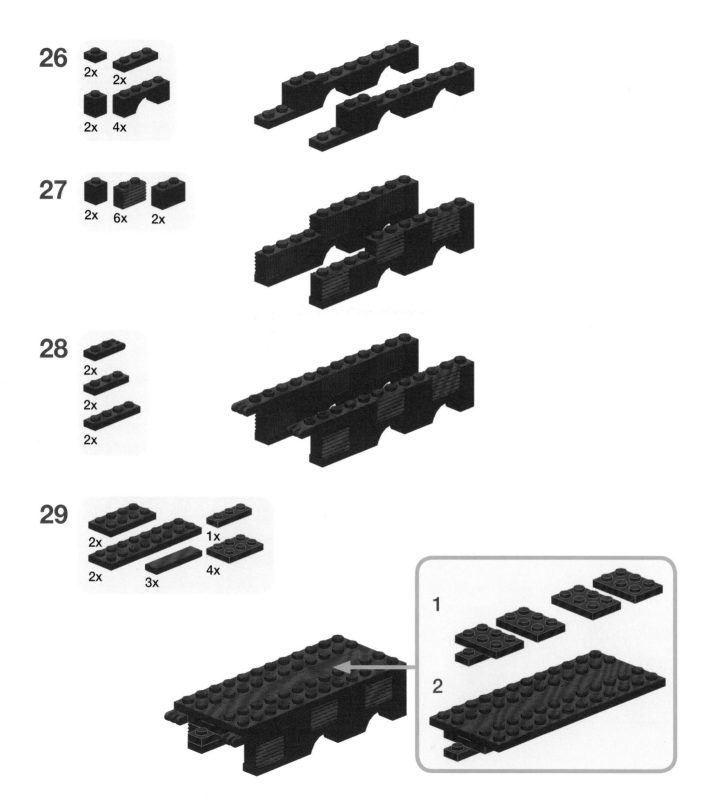

1

2

30

1x
1x
1x
1x
2x

31

2x
2x
1x
1x
2x

1
2

2x

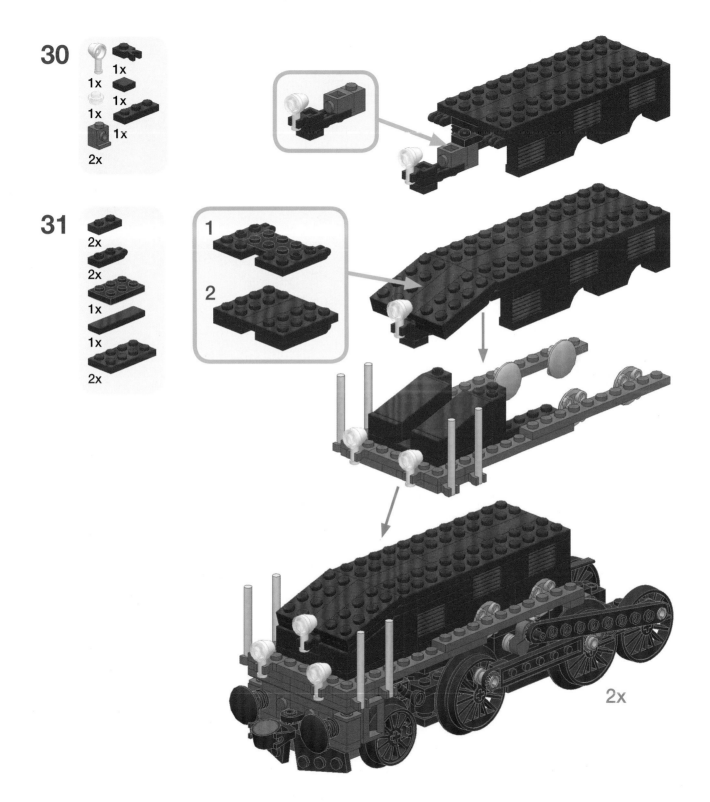

32

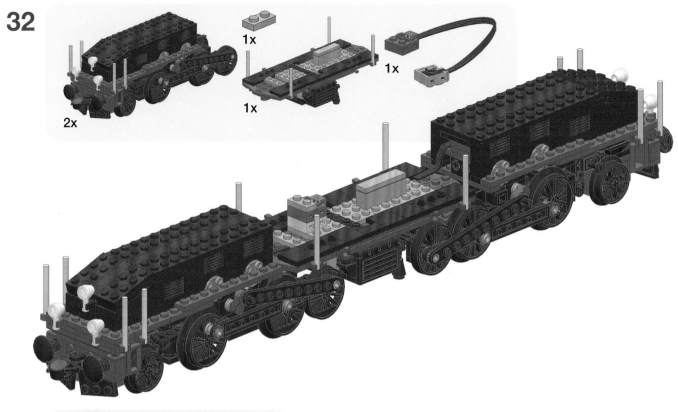

1x

2x

1x

1x

33

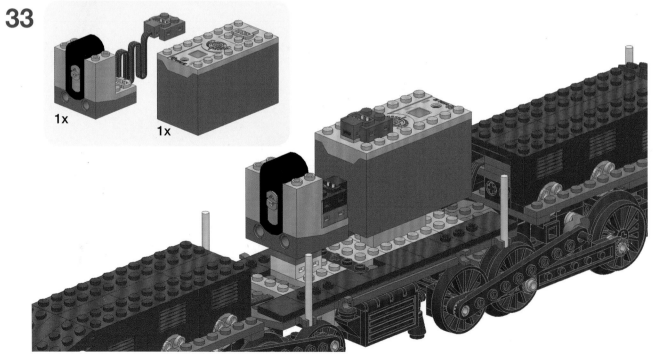

1x

1x

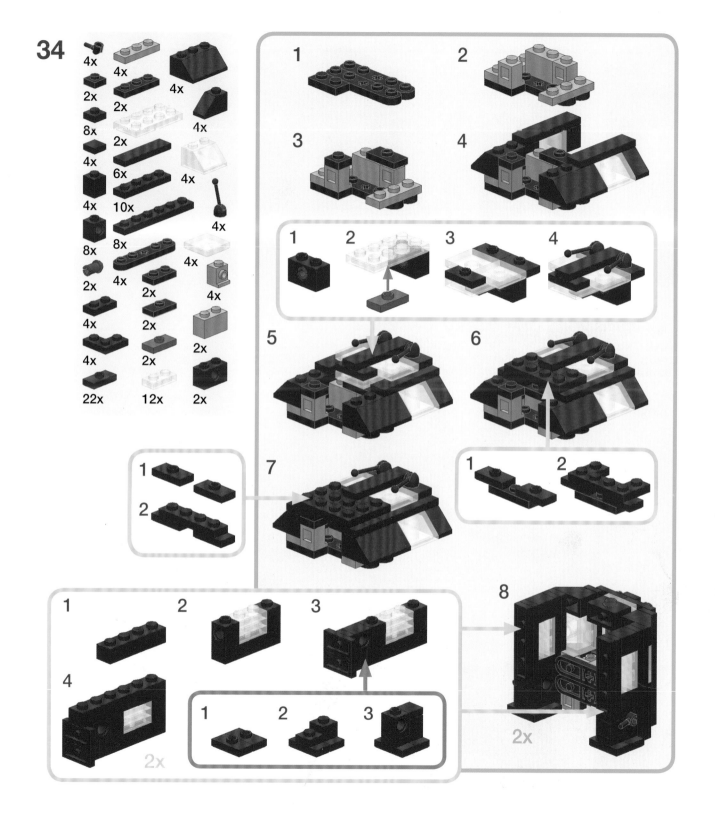

35

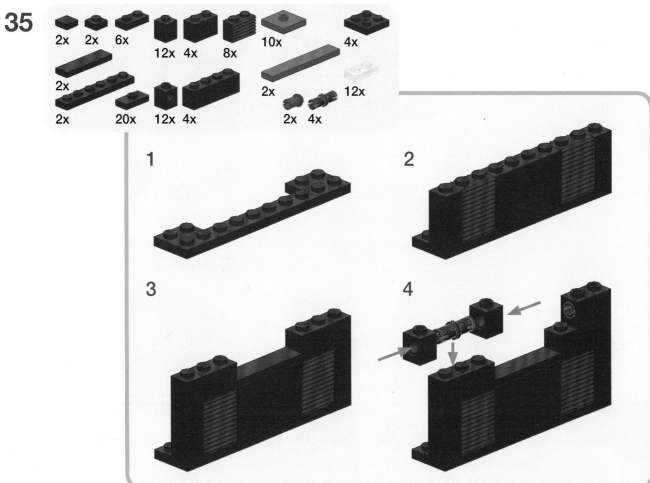

2x 2x 6x
12x 4x 8x
10x
4x

2x
2x
2x 20x 12x 4x
2x
12x
2x 4x

1 2

3 4

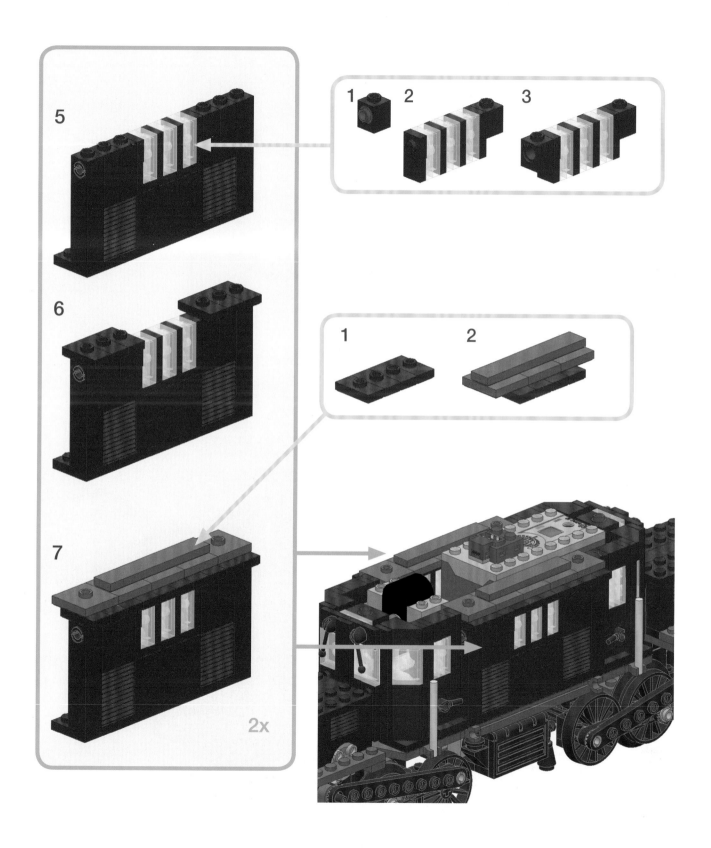

36

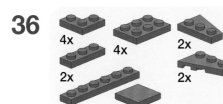

4x 4x 2x

2x 2x

4x 4x

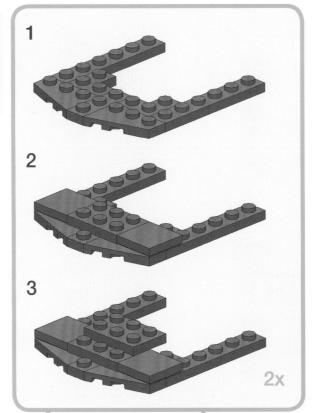

1

2

3

2x

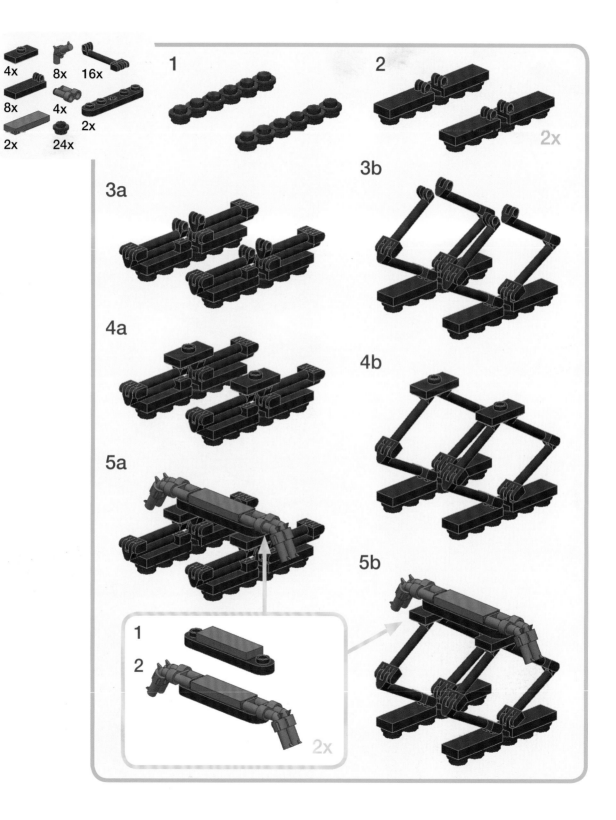

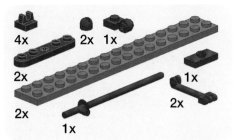

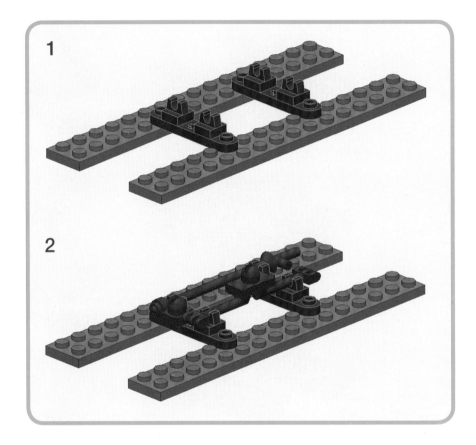

39

1x

1x

1x

VINTAGE PASSENGER CAR

FACT SHEET

Inspiration: This vintage passenger car isn't based on any particular real-world train. I was inspired by various skirted cars.

Difficulty level: Easy

Style: 7-wide

Notes:

- Dark colors make the train look somber, but a gold stripe along the side brightens things up and gives the car a classy look.

- If you want seven windows on each side, you can reduce the pillars between each window to be 1 stud wide.

- Consider playing around with the interior layout so minifigs can actually sit inside.

- To make the instructions easier to follow, all dark green parts have been drawn in tan.

- All parts in the car's main color are listed separately in the instructions.

The chrome gold lampshades are hard to find these days, so you might have to change the color or use a completely different lamp for the tables.

Elegant interior with chrome gold lampshades

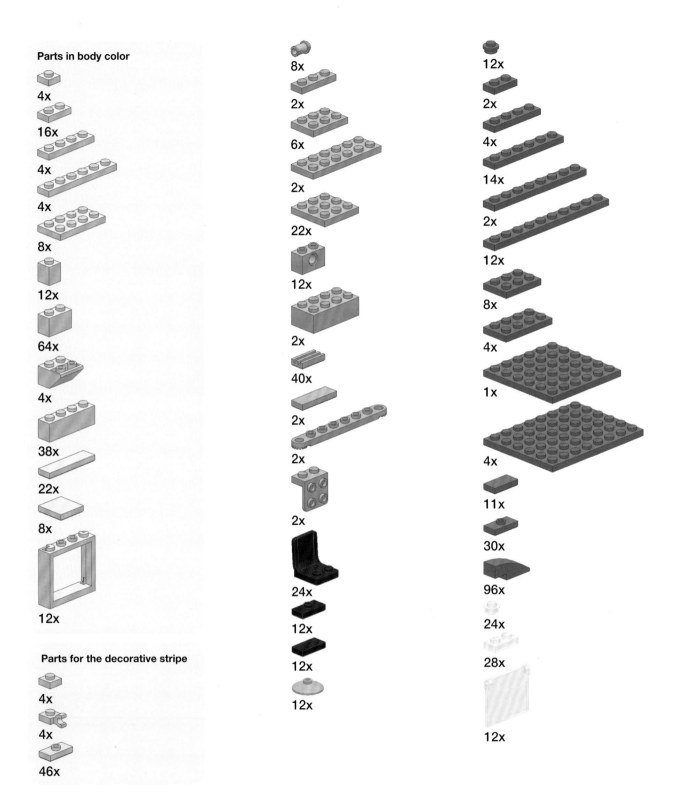

Parts in body color

4x

16x

4x

4x

8x

12x

64x

4x

38x

22x

8x

12x

Parts for the decorative stripe

4x

4x

46x

8x

2x

6x

2x

22x

12x

2x

40x

2x

2x

2x

24x

12x

12x

12x

12x

2x

4x

14x

2x

12x

8x

4x

1x

4x

11x

30x

96x

24x

28x

12x

216

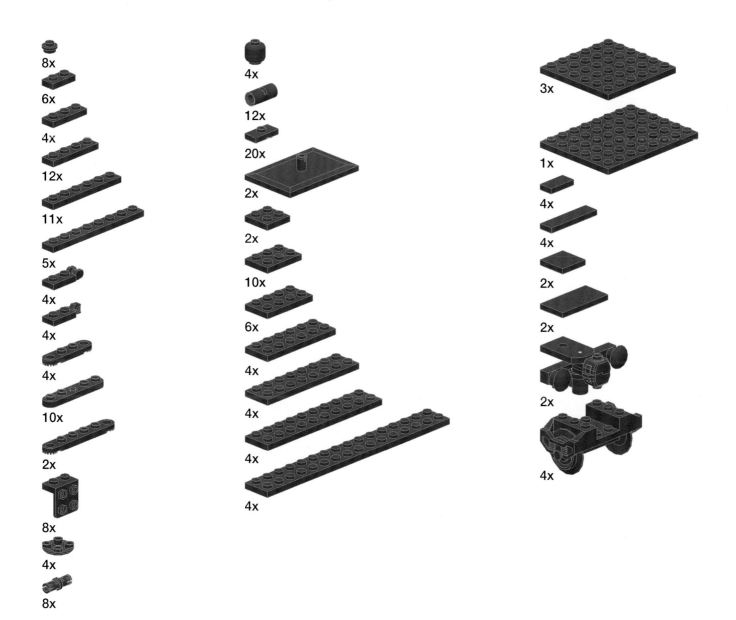

8x

6x

4x

12x

11x

5x

4x

4x

4x

10x

2x

8x

4x

8x

4x

12x

20x

2x

2x

10x

6x

4x

4x

4x

4x

3x

1x

4x

4x

2x

2x

2x

4x

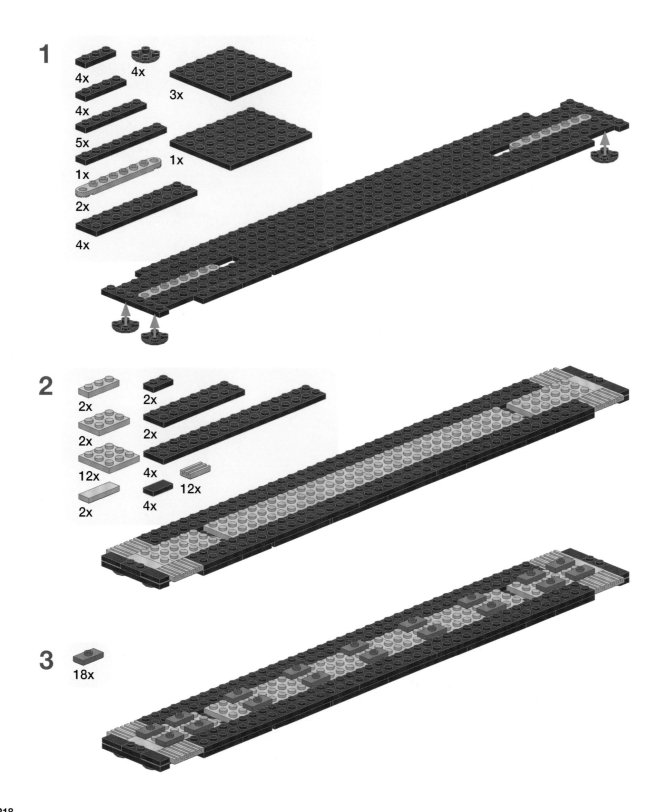

1

4x

4x

4x

4x

5x

1x

1x

1x

3x

2x

4x

2

2x

2x

2x

12x

2x

2x

2x

4x

4x

12x

3

18x

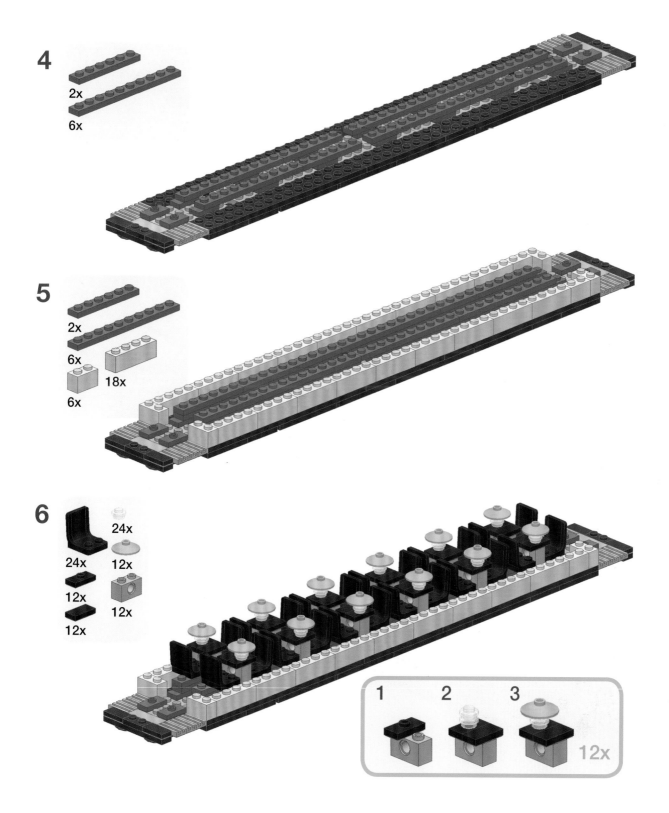

4

2x

6x

5

2x

6x

18x

6x

6

24x

24x

12x

12x

12x

12x

1   2   3

12x

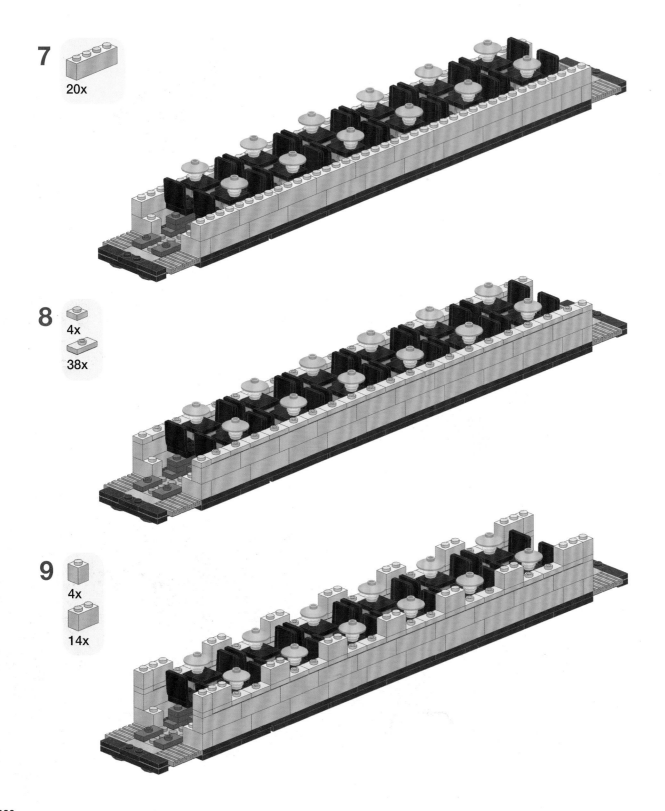

7 20x

8 4x 38x

9 4x 14x

10

4x

14x

11

4x

14x

12

12x

12x

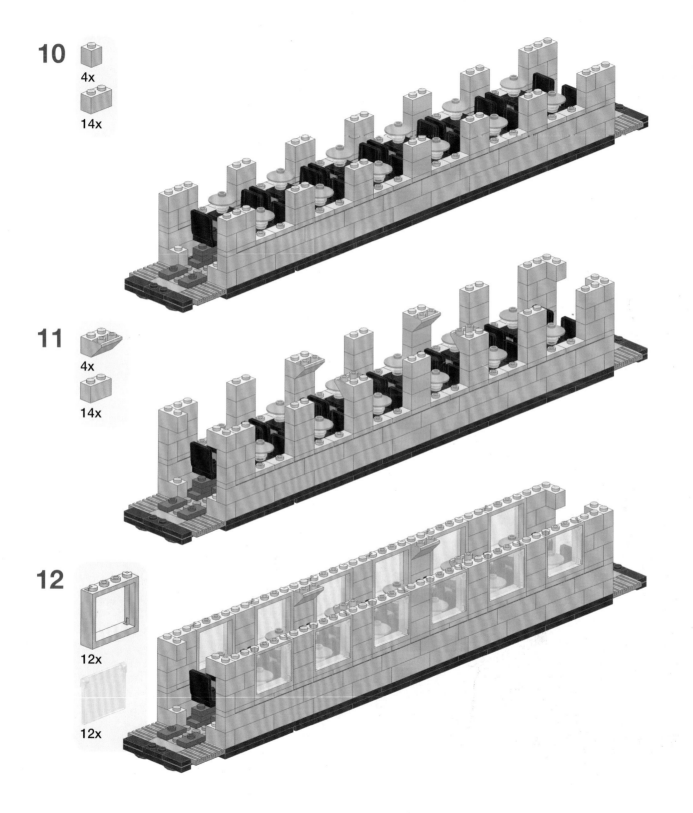

13

4x
18x
6x

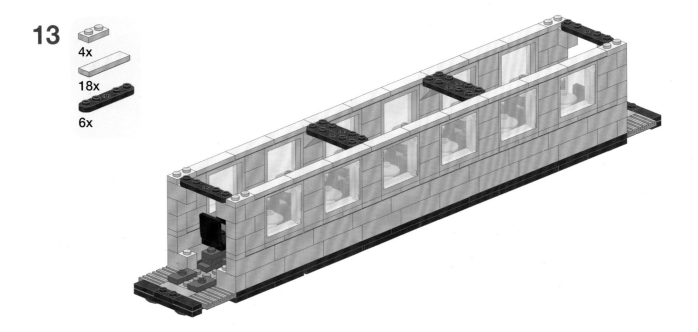

14

10x
10x
2x
4x

76x
9x

1x
10x

4x
10x

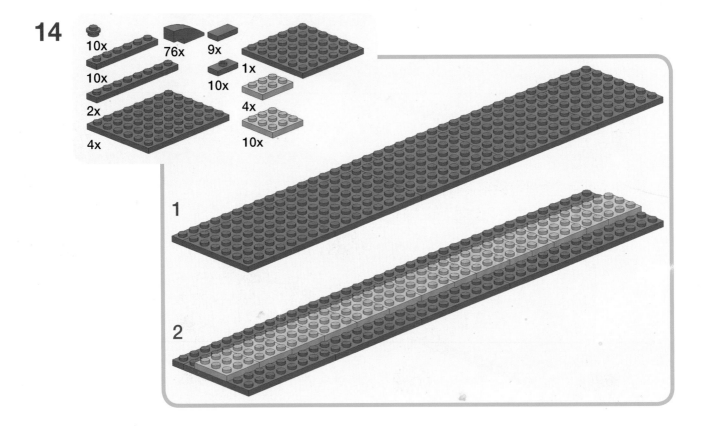

1

2

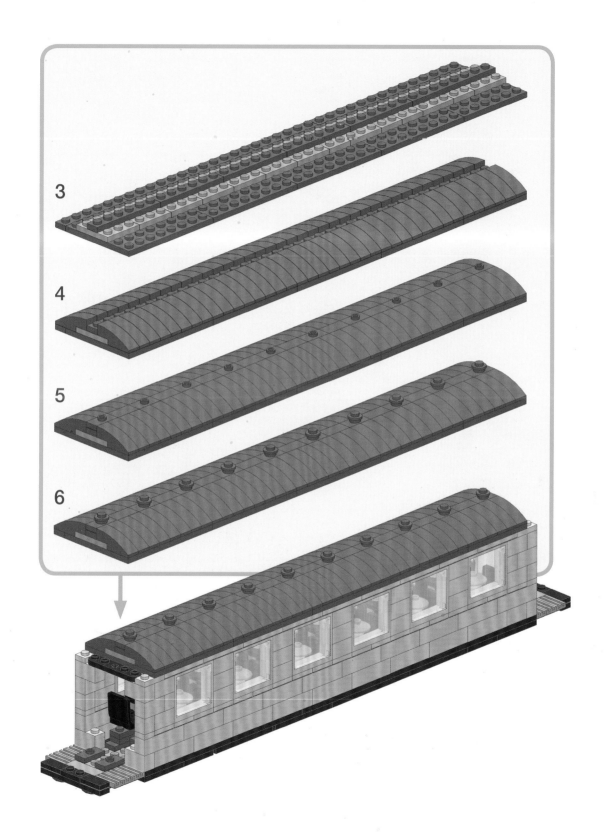

3

4

5

6

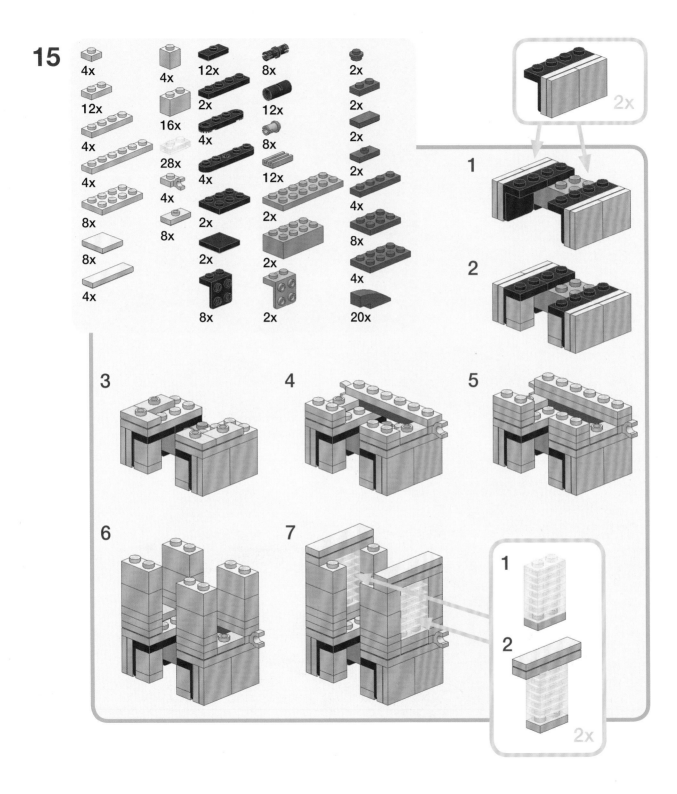

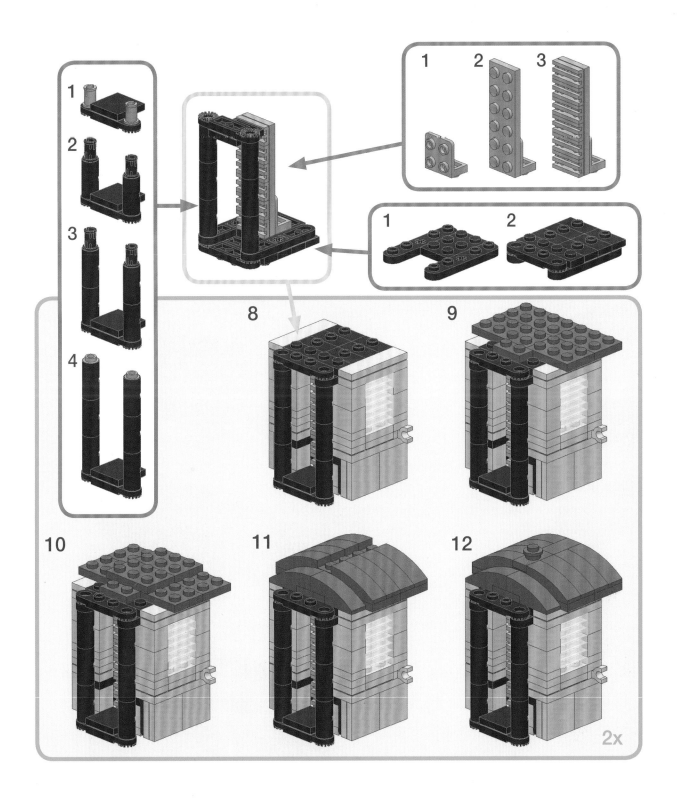

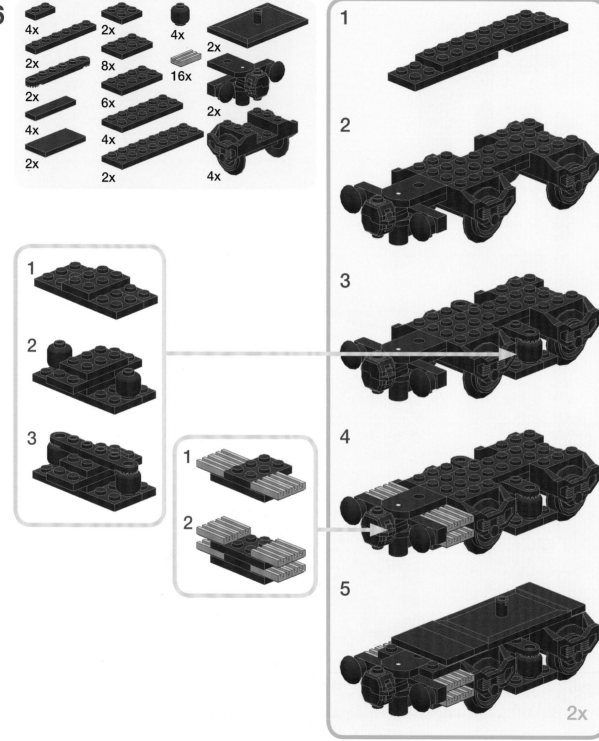

17

8x
6x
8x
4x
4x
4x
4x
2x
2x

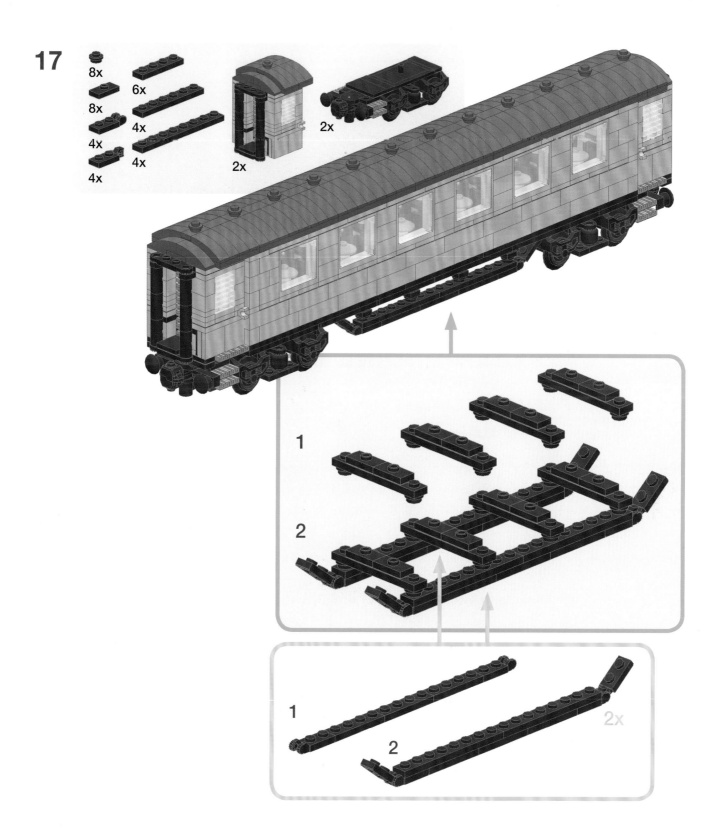

1

2

1

2

2x

Steam engine BR 80
with freight cars

STEAM ENGINE BR 80

FACT SHEET

Inspiration: Create a compact train loaded with functions.

Train type: Small steam engine with freight cars

Difficulty level: Medium to hard

Style: 8-wide

Drive: Power Functions motor, size M

Notes:

- The 1×10 Technic plates don't officially exist in red. I was lucky to find them on BrickLink one day. You can use light gray ones.

- The wheels are Big Ben Bricks, size medium, four with flange and two without.

- I put car tires around the 2×2 round bricks for the domes on top of the boiler. You'll need considerable strength and dexterity to attach them.

- I recommend using the rechargeable battery (#8878), rather than the normal battery box with 6 AAA batteries, because you don't have to remove the rechargeable one from the model for charging.

- The cable salad below the cab takes some practice and patience to put in.

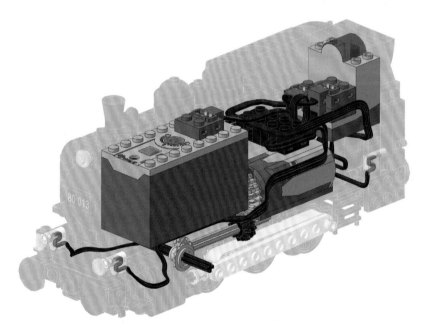

Power Functions motor and cable salad in the BR 80

BUILDING INSTRUCTIONS FOR THE BR 80

Unfortunately, the BR 80's full instructions are too long to fit in this book, but you can download them as a PDF file from *www.nostarch.com/legotrains*.

INDEX